STANDING OVER HOME

STANDING OVER HOME

A Man's Playbook To Heal Relationships
Between Fathers and Sons

Dennis Powell

Tampa, Florida

STANDING OVER HOME:
A Man's Playbook To Heal Relationships Between Fathers and Sons

Published by Gatekeeper Press
7853 Gunn Hwy., Suite 209
Tampa, FL 33626
www.GatekeeperPress.com

ISBN (paperback): 9781662950216
eISBN: 9781662950209

Quote References
Zaccharias (2017 online); stated, "Sin will take you farther than you want to go, keep you longer than you want to stay, and cost you more than you want to pay" (R. Zaccharias, 2017, online)

Anderson, (Author of The New Jim Crow (2010), "Nothing has contributed more to the systematic mass incarceration of people of color in the United States than the War on Drugs. (Michelle Anderson, 2010)

Graham (1987 sermon); In relations to a sermon titled "Just Say No" preached live in Fargo, North Dakota in 1987 by (Dr. Billy Graham sermon.)

Bible Version References
New King James
New Living Translation

PREFACE

Standing Over Home is written to help broken sons—young men who lacked the love and direction of a father figure to heal—discover respect and learn missed lessons about love and protection that were never passed down to them during their formative years. Through the eyes of author Dennis Powell, division champion Dodger pitcher, *Standing Over Home* communicates metaphorically this picture of the importance of a father's role to stand as protector and priest over his home and family. Just as a batter "stands over home" with the battling responsibility to hit or to move the runner forward, so does a father "stand over his home" to provide for, guide, and protect his family, moving them ever forward. The book draws from the real account of a son who faced some heart-breaking tragedies in life. Since his father, who lived in the house, was not in his position as head of the household, the father's absence only lined the son's path to adulthood with setbacks. Eventually, the son found himself unprepared to lead his own family. However, the goodness of God had people positioned along the way of both the Black and White races to help him discover some of the principles he never received from his father. The book will help readers acquire knowledge and prepare them to lead their families. *Standing Over Home* introduces readers to six distinctive characters they will meet as they journey from childhood to adulthood. As a result, men will value their position as a dad, be able to execute their God-given duties more effectively in the home, and forgive their father for not being there for them in their time of need.

ACKNOWLEDGEMENTS

There is no way I could have gotten to this point of being an author without the support of a few special people. To my wife and greatest supporter, Brenda, you discerned my potential to be a Godly father who provides and protects the family. You also provided me with the added inspiration to share my story with others. Thank you. To my editor and voice of correction, Ms. Sharon N. Elliott, thank you for all you have advised, added, and corrected on this project. Last but not least, thank you to all my Pastors (Pastor Diego Mesa, The late Pastors Thomas and Elzena Medlock, and The late Elder Jack Billingslea) who taught me the Word of God in a manner that I could receive and thereby grow to be a Godly leader, husband, and father.

ENDORSERS

Dennis has masterfully written something that is beyond simply a book. It is a life-skill manual about navigating the difficulties of being a professional athlete, husband, father, Christian man, and more. He has penned the words like a well-experienced writer that any best-selling author would envy. This is likely because of his humility, transparency, and often overlooked quality of authenticity that shines throughout the pages of this book. This is more than a professional athlete's biography; it is a book that any everyday man or woman can read, understand, and apply in his or her vocation or state in life. As Dennis weaves his league experiences throughout the book, readers will feel as if they were with him in a major league stadium. He writes about his childhood and how he was raised, his father's role in his life, and growing up with three brothers. He writes about the influence of male leadership that should not be overlooked within a family. He includes biblical principles he learned to depend on, which have brought him through personal struggles and temptations. He is quick to tell readers what he did right and wrong. He leaves the reader informed, inspired, and encouraged. After reading this book, I don't believe Dennis's greatest attribute or accomplishments were merely his career in professional baseball. With love and grace, he is pouring himself into a generation that can glean from his success as a leader. His story is a legacy that will impact the lives of many in a powerful way. Well done, Dennis.

—Pastor Diego Mesa
Founding Pastor, Abundant Living Family Church

. . .

Even as a Major baseball pitcher, money and success can get a man's priorities out of line. After such a neglected start to life, Dennis does a great job talking about his wake-up call to neglect, fatherhood, and God's priorities for his life. Thanks, Dennis, *Standing Over Home* is a thought-provoking book."

—Orel Hershiser
Three-time All-Star-MLB record-holder and Dodger L.A.
Dodger Analyst

. . .

After reading *Standing over Home*, I am not surprised to hear the success story of Dennis Powell. He has always had that loving spirit, an engaging smile, and that commitment to excellence. I've watched firsthand as he has stood through difficulties, yet he always smiled through it. But as is the beauty of life, it's not how you start but the impact we have on others as we grow. I never knew the depth and anguish he endured and overcame until I read

Standing over Home. Now, I know, it was his faith in God that brought him through. This world needs more men like Dennis.

—Harold Reynolds
Sports Analyst MLB Network- Former Major league Player

. . .

During my time as General Manager of the Los Angeles Dodgers, Dennis Powell was always available to help, care for, and be a blessing to people. I could sense he was a man of God. One of the strongest points of his journey is the immense value he learned about being physically available as a leader of the family. In *Standing Over Home*, he illustrates the life-changing values of being with family and being present in their lives. His book is the remarkable and real-life story of why he is who he is and why he cares so deeply.

—Ned Colletti
Former MLB Executive and General Manager of the LA Dodgers,
Author *The Big Chair*

. . .

Standing Over Home is a Great encounter of God's divine imprint on a young man who became God's man. Dennis' journey will inspire you.

—Pastor Daniel Vasquez
Senior Pastor at Calvary Chapel Summit Church

To my late father Bennie L. Powell

And To All the Men who make up the Powell lineage,
starting with my deceased brothers, Benny Lee,
Jimmy, Calvin, and Ulysee.

THE IMPETUS

On the morning of March 27, 2012, at age 49, I walked through the opened gates onto the centerfield grass of Dodger Stadium. The air seemed electric with excitement. There on the outfield, a stage had been set up facing three sections of perfectly aligned white chairs. Reporters were taking pictures as Dodger greats— Tommy Lasorda, Don Newcomb, Maury Wills, and two-time batting champion Tommy Davis—moved about the front row shaking hands and talking with dignitaries. Seated behind them were three of the four famed Dodger infielders: Steve Garvey, Ron Cey, and Davey Lopes. My seat was in the third row where I took my place, amazed to be included among a host of Dodger greats. We were all there to witness the final exchange of team ownership from Frank McCourt to the Guggenheim Management Group.

Moments later, we all heard the most recognizable voice in Dodger baseball history, Vin Scully, come over the microphone asking everyone to take their seats. He spoke about the event, and then he announced one by one, each new owner seated on the stage as well as each former player in attendance. Next, he announced NBA legend Earvin "Magic" Johnson. As Magic spoke of the privilege, ease, and honor he had with his decision to become part of the prestigious Dodger brand, my eyes unexpectedly filled with tears. Magic's words awoke a sense of honor within me that had laid dormant for years. After such a neglected childhood, I had grown up to pitch for one of the greatest organizations in professional sports, the Los Angeles Dodgers. An organization that had rostered most notably, Jackie Robinson to break the color barrier in professional baseball, and other such greats as Drysdale, Koufax, Hershiser, and Valenzuela. While I sat there bursting with this newfound energy and excitement, I couldn't help thinking about some of the other high and low points of life which had ushered me from the dusty dirt roads of Norman Park, Georgia, to the perfectly formed clay mounds inside Dodger stadium. I knew I had to share my story.

TABLE OF CONTENTS

CHAPTER 1

Are You Ready?

Train up a child in the way he should go:
and when he is old, he will not depart from it.
—Proverbs 22:6 NKJ

Hey Powell, are you ready?

It was Sunday, July 7, 1985, I will never forget that day.

Inside Busch Stadium in St. Louis, MO, the temperature was more than 102 degrees on the Astroturf. Our usual player chatter was interrupted when the bullpen phone rang, then I heard coach say, "Powell get ready." I grabbed my glove, chugged a cup of water, and hustled to the mound to start warming up. Before long, my heart was pumping as if I had just received a shot of adrenalin. I did not know if it was fear or excitement. Moments after I had thrown about twenty pitches, the phone rang simultaneously to coach hollering, "Are you ready?"

"Just a few more!" I nervously replied.

It had taken some time but all the instructions my prior coaches had voiced and demonstrated had become evident with my rapid climb through the minors. They themselves had undergone a lot of training to enjoy the benefits, privilege, and honor that comes from being a coach and seeing their work mature through my development and promotion.

After relaying my response to the manager, he quickly signaled the catcher from the dugout, prompting him to walk out to the mound where he stood casually talking, and stalling until the umpire came out and broke up the meeting. As everyone headed back to their positions, the manager's head popped up out of the dugout and he started towards the mound. Then, my bullpen coach uttered those words every rookie wants to hear, "You're in kid."

The current pitcher was relieved after throwing his warmup pitches to start the bottom of the seventh. That short delay gave me just enough time to mentally prepare myself. It was the day I would pitch in my first major league game for the Los Angeles Dodgers. I had been in the minors for two short seasons grooming for this moment. I was ready.

That debut had all the similarities as the day of my birth, except, my parents didn't have the luxury of signaling the doctor to stall my delivery. Ready or not, the time for me to make my entrance into the world had come. I arrived just like all the other babies, technically a rookie, innocent, ignorant, and crying. Once all the newborn excitement between my parents faded, the duty of gradually teaching the rules of society fell squarely on the shoulders of my father—my coach for life.

For any little boy, his father is the ultimate role model, and mine was no different. Regrettably, during my childhood, my dad was prepared for his personal pursuits of work and play; however, those pursuits distracted him from the preparation he needed to teach or even spend time with his boys. Why should a child suffer hardships, trauma, rejection, and mental anguish because the father in the relationship is not proficient enough to deal with the precious gift of life he helped create? The carelessness that I witnessed in him all those years became contagious. Consequently, as I aged, I acquired some of the same characteristics my father exhibited to me and my three older brothers. For years, I wandered around acquiring knowledge that I now know is the wrong way, by enduring hard-learned lessons and making countless mistakes. This was a life-experience I never wanted to pass on to my kids.

I recently saw a poster on the wall of a dental office, which seemed to be a microcosm of what had gone on in my family and society for decades. It read, "You don't have to brush all your teeth, just the ones you want to keep." That saying made me think of my childhood. My parents didn't have to watch all their children, just the ones

> What we neglect, we will eventually lose, and the Lord knows, I didn't want to lose any of my children.

they wanted to keep. What we neglect, we will eventually lose, and the Lord knows, I didn't want to lose any of my children.

Although my father was present in the home while I was growing up, he didn't realize he was losing his sons by his lack of involvement with us. If we had been teeth, we technically were "never brushed" and we would have been getting dangerously close to falling out. I draw attention to the actions of my father more than those of my mother because according to the Bible, a man is assigned the position as the head in a household. The roles men play within the family structure and in society are invaluable. Within the family unit, the man has the privileged task of protecting, supporting, and guiding his loved ones through life's uncertainties. If for any reason, he neglects his fatherly duties, the risk of losing one of his children increases. Growing up without a father's participation has proven to have a significant impact on children, not just on their standard of living but also their mental health and how they view the world. This unbalanced perspective can lead them down dark paths like others who face similar situations. Does any of this sound familiar?

In 2020, the US Census noted that there were 18.3 million kids raised in fatherless homes. I note this because although my father was present in the home, his involvement was as though he did not live there physically or emotionally. As a result, my brothers and I made a lot of mistakes. Now, as a man, who is also a father, I believe the number of us fleeing our responsibilities will not change until we start holding ourselves more accountable by confronting our pride and the identity crisis within. We as fathers need to recognize the negative impact we are adding to lives of our son(s). When we can't provide for our family, we see our-selves as failures. If we don't address the mental and physical pressures facing us as men, then we will continue to take flight rather than stay and fight. Staying in the fight just for sake of the children and marriage is more about changing us, than us changing our circumstances.

After I reached the professional ranks, I learned how to break the game down to one inning, one batter, one pitch at a time. I did not think about the fourth batter of the game until I powered through the first, second, and third one. This mindset gave me a better chance to succeed. I believe if we're going to change the plight of absent men in the home like my father, then we must change them through training and supporting one man at a time.

Ironically, baseball sets up the perfect metaphor to many of the occurrences that happened to my family and me. My story is not only a tale about baseball; it is also my account of negligent acts, which eventually forced this major league pitcher to reposition his posture, not as a batter; but as a father. Professional baseball is the game that carried me around the world, but it is also a sport that took me away from time with my family. On average, I spent nine to ten months abroad, going to spring training, and traveling to places like the Dominican Republic, Colombia, Venezuela, Mexico, and Japan to earn better wages and improve my skills.

While I developed myself as a pitcher, my wife stood at home, fulfilling my role as father, priest, and head of household. She was also the one who was responsible for our children's discipline and nurturing in the early stages of their lives.

Nevertheless, something happened one off-season that caught my attention. My five-year old daughter Nicole innocently asked my wife, Brenda, "Is daddy going to spend the night?"

I had been in and out of the house so much pursuing my profession that my fatherly rights and basic skills had all but disappeared. Throughout my return to Mexico for the season, her inquiry reverberated in my mind like a terrible song playing over and over. The burdening weight of her question pushed me to think more about my responsibilities as a father.

Although I put up team-leading statistics while in Mexico, I sensed it would be the last team I would play for in my baseball career. While I was not experientially and spiritually ready, the time had arrived for me to take my rightful place as the head of the family. The commitment of fatherhood would be one of the most privileged obligations I would undertake in my life.

It wasn't until I began walking in the role of a father, that I realized how untrained I was to lead and protect my own family. In Proverbs 22:6, the word of God cautions those in charge to "train up a child in the way that he should go: and when he is old he will not depart from it" (NKJ). This proverb is a warning to parents and not a promise. Nevertheless, I believe some of my early shortcomings and fears about adulthood could have been reduced if Dad—my coach for life—had been there to take a more established stance with his time and showing me how to develop a relationship with God. Regardless, there were still a lot of particulars I did not know concerning how to be a man.

Fathers, we have a responsibility not only to ready our sons born into our care, to one-day stand on their own, but to also support and encourage them just as a coach would his players. I didn't know how to handle adversity, take responsibility, deal with life, tie a tie, shave, handle relationships, open a bank account or just show love because Dad didn't take the time to teach me about those areas.

Throughout my minor league baseball career, my managers would leave me in the game during critical stretches because I was the type of pitcher who could always pitch my way out of a jam. This sort of trust from my coaches came from years of me re-examining and reprocessing both good and bad games. Reprocessing was simply me using past experiences, decisions, information, and results to confront present predicaments. Ironically, it was this same course of action that helped me expose and break a generational curse that had lingered in my biological family for years. Through the application of God's Word and by reprocessing many hard learned lessons, I finally realized, after years of wandering, how to stand up as a man and give God the broken pieces of my past, so that He could make me whole. This decision not only changed how I viewed life, but it also empowered me to face it. God is the One Source who was able to break the pattern of neglect and rebellion which had reigned in my family line for decades. Yet, it would require more than human strength to hold on to this new revelation. It took the Holy Spirit and total surrender. Psalms 124:2-3 declares, "If it had not been the LORD who was on our side, when men rose up against us: Then they would have swallowed us alive (NKJ)." Whether we acknowledge Him or not, God is the deciding factor behind our success.

Within my story, the harsh realities of life emerge as over-powering pitches coming from the hand of a pitcher. Although some tragedies struck early, the ensuing after-effects rippled through my adult years. The piercing strikes which battered my family came from various angles and in different forms. The over-powering effects of alcohol, drugs, and ignorance presented many setbacks for me and my family. Not only did this deadly trio hijack my childhood, but they also revealed other hidden weaknesses within me along the way. Over time, I believed being ill-equipped to handle life's curves derailed my professional career. My story reveals how life will openly administer consequences and pain-fully teach the rules our fathers neglected to hand-out or address. Parts of my story will make you laugh, while pieces of it are heartfelt and might make you cry.

In this game called life, I had to choose a side to stand on, but for many of the earlier years, I wavered. God was speaking to me the whole time, yet I chose to focus on my own selfish pursuits. I positioned myself on the side of doubt and unbelief. I promoted and talked about God, but I did not follow or walk in His principles. I foolishly believed I controlled my every move and that there were no such things as spiritual forces; stuff just happened. Have you ever assumed such a foolish thing?

Men, no matter how many times you've failed with your families, God wants you to know He can change that cycle of failure because He has never lost a battle. You can taste victory if you stop running from challenges. For men who feel alone and tired of running away from broken relationships plagued with unfulfilled promises, I pray you will keep reading. Likewise, men who feel like you have it all together, I also implore you to read on. Keep in mind, one piece of unsuspecting news could be the pitch that knocks you to your knees. The word of God holds the keys to freedom if we would just trust Him.

Now, come along with me as I share a few landslide victories and some heartbreaking losses, which I hope will help you stand and be the man or father, God has called you to be.

CHAPTER 2

Home Alone

Likewise, exhort the young men to be
sober minded, in all things showing yourself
to be a pattern of good works…
—Titus 2:6 NKJ

In sports, having home-field advantage can sometimes be the difference between the team scoring a win or a loss. Some of the best games I've ever pitched came from the cheers and positive vibes of hometown fans and my teammates. Their energy and belief somehow pushed me to a higher level of sheer confidence, command, and control. The pressure of pitching at home or on the road didn't overwhelm me because I had been trained for the big moment by coaches and trainers. Just as my coaches had assisted me in baseball, my parents held the same burden to get me ready to stand and face life both at home and as I aged. I am experienced and old enough to tell you now, I wasn't mentally or experientially ready to leave when I left home.

When I imagine a home and the benefits that reside there, I see a safe, comfortable place filled with uplifting love and support. Since mom did all she could to nurture her boys, the home I grew up in had some of the above-mentioned elements, but it came up short in many of the others because mom wasn't created to teach me how to be a man. That was my father's responsibility.

This one-sided style of parenting reminded me of the kid in the movie *Home Alone* who had to fend for himself after his family forgot to take him on their Christmas vacation. The kid had to protect himself against those who wanted to do mischief. In somewhat the same way, my brothers and I were left to fend for ourselves. Therefore, the home alone I want to talk about is not exactly like the theme of the movie. No, the home alone I want to discuss is when a father thoughtlessly leaves his sons mentally and physically alone with the mother to learn life's dos and don'ts on their own.

Years after my major league career ended, I came across an amazingly helpful book titled *Is There a Man in the House* written by Carlton Pearson. It highlights that presence doesn't always mean "in attendance." Dad was proof of this fact, home in the body but absent in involvement.

I grew up about 175 miles south of Atlanta, Georgia, in a little rural town called Norman Park. The population in 1970 was close to eight hundred and ninety-one, with twenty percent of that number being African American. Out of the two houses we had lived in, I remember the twelve hundred square foot, two-bedroom home right off Highway-319 the most. I remember it well because the house would tremble with the passing of each semi-tractor trailer truck. To accommodate each member, my parents placed their bed in the small living room section, my grandmother occupied a room, while my three brothers and I had two beds side by side in the other small room.

As far back as I can recall, Dad had only missed one day on the job; his work ethic was impeccable. When he worked in the pulp-wooding industry, we knew when he was home simply by the smell of pine sap blowing off his clothes and seeping through the screen door into the house. Around age eight, I remember the exciting stir around the house when dad made the transition from pulp-wooding to construction. Leaving pulp-wooding was a welcomed change, but it also came with unforeseen costs.

Dad's new job was an upgrade financially, plus it gave mom relief from having to wash his sappy clothes. His new work-crew normally picked him up in front of the house at about five o'clock in the morning and dropped him off around five-thirty in the afternoon. His routine after that was to bathe, eat, watch television, and go straight to bed. Sometimes when the commute was too far, dad's crew left on a Monday with their suitcases and did not return until Friday. This unpredictable schedule of going out of town went on and off for well over twenty-five years. During these long hours away from home, my brothers and I had to pay the startling price of figuring out life for ourselves.

One morning jumps to mind giving you an example of how things functioned in our house. The weather in South Georgia had a routine all its own. Most days started off hot and humid, and then like clockwork in the early afternoon, a thunderstorm usually rolled in. As brilliant streaks of sunlight pierced through the cracks in the curtains, I snuggled into dad's oversized recliner waiting for Saturday morning cartoons to start. My nose was being treated to the savory smell of pork sausage, bacon, eggs, and grits gently wafting out of Mom's kitchen. Cooking a big breakfast was her routine on the weekends. Otherwise, Rice Krispies or Sugar Frosted Flakes would have been on the menu.

"Dent, tell your brothers to get up; it's time to eat."

Dent was a nickname that stuck with me after a misguided attack with some friends. After chasing this elusive squirrel up into a tree and surrounding it, a hailstorm of rocks ensued. The next thing I saw was a flash of light and then darkness. A launched half-brick by one of my friends at the squirrel came down and hit me right in the center of my skull for the knock-out. To this day, a dimple remains. It's a present-day reminder of some painful blows that knocked me down but did not keep me down.

As I leaned over the arm of the chair, pulled back the curtains that separated the two rooms, the room unexpectedly darkened, as I yelled "Get up, it's time to eat,". Next, I dashed to the front door to see what was happening. I got there just in time to witness storm clouds that had surprisingly rolled in and blocked out the sun. Out of nowhere, there was a thunderous boom and a sharp flash of lightning that sent my heart into overdrive as it chased me back to my seat.

Mom shouted, "Dent, turn off that television."

I remember always having to superstitiously shut off certain electrical appliances during thunderstorms. Just like that, my date with the "Bugs Bunny Road Runner Hour" came to a screeching halt.

I could hear mom grumbling, "Maybe that will put an end to all that noise and digging coming from those workers across the road."

"Dent, come get your plate, it's on the table." As I got my plate and headed back to my seat, the bottom appeared to have dropped out of the sky. The rain came down all at once; hitting and running off the windows so hard, I could not even see outside.

"Wow! It's really coming down," I said.

"Who cares? Get out of the way," my brother screeched.

Benny Lee wanted the recliner I was sitting in since Dad wasn't home to claim it. Although I put up some resistance, he soon got his wish. Luckily, I had already gotten my breakfast from the kitchen because my other two brothers, Calvin, and Jimmy, were also up.

"Save your father something to eat," yelled mom. My three brothers were known for annihilating everything edible in sight like a pack of ravenous wolves.

Benny Lee was the oldest of my three brothers. He resembled a towering flagpole swaying in the wind. His tall, wiry frame was always tilting forward. There were moments he would flash the skills and talents of the sports star people had predicted he would become. Then, there were times the police would knock at the door. Sometimes they came with questions and other times they came with an eyewitness account of his suspected involvement and a subsequent arrest. As he aged, his talent and dreams slowly faded away because of his off-the-field activities—partying, girls, drugs, and run-ins with the law.

Jimmy was the second oldest and the most dependable of my siblings. He was a proven basketball player and a pure hitter in baseball whose talents faded in the same manner as our older brother. After graduation, he took a job with the Department of Transportation while fathering four beautiful kids with his girlfriend.

Then there was Calvin; he was the shortest of my brothers and yes, he was also good at sports. Well-groomed, polite, and generous, that was Calvin. Jimmy and my brother Calvin were equal when it came to showing respect. Between all four of us, Calvin had the biggest heart, but a heart without God is still capable of unexplained actions. All three enjoyed life and had fun. Calvin would give you the shirt off his back. Yet his biggest problem came in the form of peer pressure. Over time, his athletic skills faltered like the others.

And then there was me. I was Dennis the Menace; a stuttering, little sandy-haired boy who terrorized the streets by throwing rocks at streetlights until they were broken. I hid in ditches beside the highway just to throw rocks at passing semi-trailer trucks, causing some drivers to occasionally pull over. I would often knock on the doors of the older folks, and then run to hide before they answered the door. While dad slept, I took cigarettes from the pack, only to go light up and puff with my friend. Some have said, "I could steal the sweetener out of sugar I was so slick."

Unfortunately, all the signs of neglect, attitude build-up, and our declining morals never shifted Dad's routine. Dad kept going to work every day, seemingly oblivious to all the mischief and negative changes into which we boys—his sons—were sinking daily. Like those teeth mentioned earlier, we were getting looser and looser, more and more rotten, yet Dad never brushed and flossed us—never paid attention to the fact that he could be losing us to the world.

Because I am a father of four today, I know there were certain things I messed up with my first son that I achieved with my other kids. As I considered my father's limited dealings with us, I noticed he kept up his normal activities every Friday after cashing his check from a long work week. Regardless of his devotion to work, it was his customary trip to a section of town we called "the Quarters" which filled his spare time. The man who left was not the same one who returned. After long hours away drinking, he would sometimes return drunk. On many occasions, I witnessed his drunken fury as he punched or verbally attacked mom for no reason. His lack of respect for mom, not only angered and weakened me as a young man, but it also left me feeling unprotected and unloved as I allowed my surroundings to shape me. Dad easily dished out punishment when he was around, but sitting, listening to our concerns, and trying to connect with us about life and the pressures of being a man never happened. Living without the constant and positive influences of a father made it easy for me to pick up the everyday practices I saw in others throughout the neighborhood.

In fact, as I grew, I saw behaviors of a home-alone kid in each of my older brothers. We were all about self-happiness. In other words, we made choices based on whether or not we would be happy or satisfied. Selfishness was the order of the day. This is what we had seen and been taught; do for yourself. As a result, my brothers started showing little respect for females. They started treating girls as paths to self-gratification. They unemotionally dated them and used them as toys to partake in their amusement. Once they were bored or unsatisfied with them, they discarded them without any attachment.

One reason for their precarious lifestyles is that we didn't have good male representation. We grew up seeing lots of disrespect towards women in the form of domestic violence, shacking, fornication, and adultery. Men regularly made babies with no real intent to commit or marry. Not to mention the violent behaviors, drinking, cursing, and gambling that was displayed by most of the men and my father on the weekends. As a kid, I saw knives and guns pulled, and men fighting with broken bottles because of something that happened in a poker or dice game. I guess in one sense, the old cliché, "like father like son," held some early truths because most of the boys I grew up with walked in the same path as their fathers.

Sure, Dad possessed notable qualities when it came to working, but still he struggled to score points with his sons by neglecting to end the long cycle of abuse within the home. Because of this, the relationship between my father and his sons continued to separate.

A huge thunderclap and bright lightening flash brought my mind back to the Saturday morning scene at hand.

Although it continued to rain throughout most of the afternoon, the lightning finally ceased, so I was able to get back to watching television. However, by this time, my cartoons were over, and my second favorite type of television show was now on—Westerns. The earsplitting sound of the bugle-man's horn always pulled me to the edge of my seat as the Calvary came charging down the hillside to rescue the people inside the burning fort. As a kid, I always wondered why the Indians ignited the tips of their arrows with fire before shooting them into the fort's wooden walls. I later understood that they deliberately shot flaming arrows to create confusion. The fiery arrows also posed a serious threat to the walls if no one snuffed out the flames.

Satan had been strategically using this same tactic on my family. He had been unleashing flaming arrows of neglect, busyness, anger, pride, depression, and alcohol into the walls of our home. While dad's attention focused on the pursuit of his own pleasures, these smoldering arrows were rapidly spreading their fire and burning out of control within our lives. One of a father's main responsibilities is to protect those entrusted to him. Since a father cannot be with his sons everywhere they go, then he must support and equip them with the necessary skills to survive.

As a kid, I was given basic right and wrong directives, but visual communication and demonstration is what spoke the loudest to me. I needed a more balanced picture to go with the verbal. It was hard to restrain the wildness and foolishness in my heart with simple "do as I say and not as I do" commands. For extended periods of time, I was alone to make my own determinations. Many men today are still stuck mentally as home alone boys in a youthful state because their fathers never came rushing to the rescue like the Calvary. Consequently, their little boys have grown into men who still play immature and childish games, who in turn function as models for their own kids and the cycle continues. Now, each generation wanders around living out the experiences that were modeled for them. Every day, many men get up repeating the same sequence of mistakes demonstrated to them, while fighting against anything or anyone that gets in their way. They use the "by any means necessary" mentality to keep afloat. By that, I mean they throw the moral rulebook out the door just to find a temporary fix.

My dad never established a father-son bond with me, and years into my adulthood, I discovered the reason. He had grown up in a fatherless environment himself. I never found out why his mom was raising him alone. Tragically, she died after she fell off the back of a pickup truck, and then his maternal grandmother stepped in to raise him. My father never had the opportunity to experience a dad's love for his son. The interactions of a healthy father-son relationship were never demonstrated for him to pass along.

At some point, the missing father issue must be corrected. We men who have become fathers basically need to show up and purposefully establish those much-needed father-son bonds. We must stand atop the walls of our homes monitoring the behavioral needs of all who dwell within. We cannot continue to turn away while our sons are left alone to deal with the fiery arrows of life's setbacks and disappointments.

We can look around at society and see that there is a male problem by the number of single women staying and raising their kids alone. Two defining factors add to this crisis: men in prison, and men operating by the same poor standards with which they were raised. Since we know the justice system is slanted against us as Black men, we must start doing everything in our power to stay vigilant in our compliance with the rules of society. We men also say we will not drop the ball like our dads did, yet we end up repeating the same cycle of son-neglect, just under a different name or excuse. That is what I saw in my dad. He missed years of opportunities to break that pattern of abandonment and lead us down a new path. Consequently, his casual style of child-rearing—which meant leaving it up to Mom—had also allowed the curse of spiritual neglect to travel all the way down the family tree right into my lap.

Through the relationship I didn't have with my father, and the one I have been learning to build with my children, I've discovered five vital areas in which we can SCORE with our sons:

S = Support

We must be a major source of support in our sons' lives. My dad missed many opportunities to show me I was valuable, protected, loved, and a priority. He missed connecting and correcting the emotions I was feeling. Most of all, he missed teaching me how to respect a woman. I missed playing and talking with him about relationships and life. However, with my sons, I showed them I would be there by attending their events. I taught them to be responsible, honest, caring, respectful toward women, reverent toward God, and to never be afraid to ask for help. I showed them being vulnerable, truthful, and open is better than being self-reliant.

C = Connection (Bonding)

We must connect with our sons, bonding man-to-man with them from the time they are babies.

O = Open Ear (Communication)

We must have open ears to our sons, listening to hear what they are really going through, and communicating back that we understand and have some wisdom to share. I never had a heart-to-heart talk with my father about anything serious, whether it was sex, work, religion, education, or money.

R = Rock (Protection)

We must show ourselves as the rock of protection for our sons. If anyone has their backs, they must be assured that their father will always be there for them.

E = Educator (Mentor)

And finally, we score with our sons when we are their educator—their main mentor. Do you really want your son learning about women, sex, finance, and courage on the streets?

So, if the father in your life has left you to learn valuable lessons alone, God says, "He will never leave you nor forsake you" (Deuteronomy 31:8, NKJ). Know that the abandonment is not your fault. In addition, God holds the key and a plan to unlock your cell of pain, anger, and un-forgiveness. He has a new life for you that is full of knowledge and guidance. All you have to do to score with your sons is to sincerely ask Jesus into your heart as Lord. Then follow Him as He directs your steps, decisions, and relationship to pull you closer.

CHAPTER 3

Know the Opposition

Jesus replied, your mistake is that
you don't know the scriptures, and you
don't know the power of God.
—Matthew 22:29 NLT

In my professional seasons with the Los Angeles Dodgers, I learned various forms of communication. One applicable routine occurred before each new series when coaches, pitchers, and catchers would get together to assess the opposing players. In this setting, we discussed strategies to counter each batter's strengths and how to exploit their weaknesses. The data discussed came from in-game performances packaged by our scouting department for presentation. We learned from their report how to challenge each batter with certain pitches, locations, and defenses. This analytical approach gave our pitching staff and the team a better chance for success.

As I look back over the method the Dodger's used versus the hands-off approach my dad chose, I realized my brothers and I started off on the road to adulthood at a huge disadvantage. Although dad—my coach for life—had amassed vital firsthand information through experience, there were no father-son sit-downs which could have helped us improve our chances of success. Consequently, we had no idea who or what we were facing as we moved through our teenage and subsequent years.

As I revealed in the earlier chapter, heavy rainstorms were common in Georgia. This reflection takes me back to a weekend before we had moved when it rained so hard, Noah's Ark could have floated on groundwater. Still, that didn't stop my cousin and a couple of friends from meeting up at the corner once the rain had passed. As we strayed from the yard, we spotted a large backhoe left by the workers just across the road from home. Without any hesitation, we snooped around a little further and came across a freshly dug trench that had filled with water. Next, these floating logs in the corner which looked like a little eight to ten-foot bridge caught our attention.

Then, I heard my cousin, "Dent, I bet you three oatmeal pies you can't get across those logs."

Oatmeal pies were the magic words. All my friends knew I loved Lance Oatmeal Pies. "Jjjj…uusst www..aaatch..hh," I said.

It took a few seconds for the words to form, but my response finally made it out. Stuttering made the gang burst out in laughter. My struggle speaking manifested itself early in my childhood and has lasted well into my adult life. My stuttering is nowhere near as embarrassing now as it was back then. I remember instances in school when the teacher would call on me to answer a question. Her intentions were pure, as she only wanted to encourage me, but that approach only made matters worse. The moment she said my name, my lips clinched as if I had stuffed a hand full of peanut butter-filled crackers into my mouth. I knew what I wanted to say but it just wouldn't come out smoothly. My words got blocked at the first syllable causing the class to erupt into laughter. There were times when I literally ran out of the class in tears. Stuttering always left me as the center of jokes with my friends. I didn't like it, and neither should you who stutter. If you know someone who stutters, please do not interrupt, or try to finish their sentences. Don't say slow down, relax, or make remarks. Just give them your attention by listening, being patient, and standing with them, not against them.

After taking a couple of steps out onto the logs nothing happened, so I moved a little bit more, still nothing. Step by step, I gently slipped my foot further and further out. Then without any forewarning, the logs suddenly started to roll. Splash! I fell face first into the water. Each time I surfaced, I could hear, "Paddle your arms, Dent, paddle your arms." I recall slapping, kicking, and fighting the water until everything went dark. The last thing I remember hearing was, "Aunt Lucile, Aunt Lucile, Dent has fallen into the water!" The next voice I heard as I was lying in the mud was my mother's.

"Dent, Dent, can you hear me? Say something, are you okay? How did you get in there?"

While I gasped for air on the side of that embankment with my mom and friends looking on, I could not tell you how I made it to the edge. There was no way I was going to utter the words, "Oatmeal pies." So, I anxiously searched my mind for another answer.

"I just got too close to the edge and slipped in."

Just like that, I had openly lied to mom as my friends stood there silently agreeing. That 'slip-in' almost cost me my life. I knew I was wrong for lying, but I had learned it from the grown-ups. What type of mixed message do you think an eight-year-old receives when adults tell him drinking, lying, smoking, and fighting is bad? Then, I see them doing the very thing they told me not to do.

While walking back to the house, my friends told me what they saw. "The way you kicked and flapped your arms must have kept you floating, and the splashing kept you close to the edge where we could reach you with a short branch and pull you out."

Although I haven't talked too much about the incident since that day, it is a day I will never forget.

When I finally looked at Mom's face, I could see the concern start to ease. "Thank God you're okay." I had heard Mom utter "thank God" before, I just didn't know the omnipotence of God or His ways. That bit of spiritual information was never clearly communicated in our home. Nevertheless, as I sit here today, I know who God is and I can tell you for sure, an angel of God helped pull me out of death's grip that day.

Usually, Sunday's meant church. However, there were no strict parental demands on going to church in our family. We rarely went as a family. Some days just mom and other times maybe dad and the rest of us showed up later. Morning Grove Baptist Church was only in-service on 1st and 3rd Sundays. On 2nd and 4th Sundays, the congregation usually visited other nearby churches. The customary way the preachers sighed and moaned the sermon made it difficult for some adults to extract the message, so how do you think us kids faired? After the services, all that resonated with me was the groans of the preacher. Unsurprisingly, I never got the full gospel message in church, so that responsibility fell onto my parents to explain. Yet, sit-downs to reflect on church service were non-existent. This was one of the first opportunities in Dad's position as leader to change the culture in our family line. Nonetheless, his carelessness fell right into Satan's plan of attack. The devil's desire is to destroy lives and he doesn't care the age or how he does it. Imagine all the life-changing knowledge and strength circulating in the church towards the adults while us kids sat nearby spiritually wasting away. As parents, we can't keep dropping the ball when it comes to equipping our kids for total success.

Not too long ago, I watched a movie called *Usual Suspects*. During the police interrogation of a suspect, the main character uttered this profound statement, "The greatest trick the devil ever pulled was convincing the world he did not exist." This claim has never been truer and should inspire all humans to examine their beliefs and actions in life.

That same devilish proclamation is as true today as it was when I was a kid. At present, there are a growing number of families replacing church and spiritual development with more leisure and athletic pursuits. Travel sports teams and games have become a Sunday norm to the distraction and harm of kids who need a more solid and spiritual foundation to manage life's curves. In addition to sports, reading, writing, and arithmetic, parents should regularly set aside time to sit down and breakdown the following six key and very influential figures their kids will eventually have to contend with as they move through life. Each entity holds a well-defined position and carries significant influences whether you believe in them or not. They are God, Jesus Christ, the Holy Spirit, Satan, the flesh, and the world.

We as men must prepare our sons to stand up righteously against the world's pressures and its views. One of the most opportune places to start is by advising them on who is fighting on their side and alerting them to who is standing in opposition. This should start when they are young and continue throughout their development.

If you have gotten to this place in your life without knowing or ever having these key players' strengths and weaknesses clearly explained, let me be the first to bring you up to speed on who is who. Even though you might be off to a late start, it is not too late for you to learn about them, your purpose, and the roles they play in your life.

God

God (Colossians 1:16 NKJ) is the Creator of all things. He has set in motion a plan to recover fallen humanity from the world by sending His Son Jesus Christ to redeem man. God is omnipotent and omnipresent, which means He is all-powerful and is everywhere at the same time. Without a doubt, God is the most powerful of this group.

Jesus

While God rules all, He has placed all power into the hands of His Son, Jesus Christ (Matthews 28:18 NKJ). Without the shedding of Jesus' blood in forgiveness, our sins persist. The redeeming power of salvation is in His blood.

The Holy Spirit

When Jesus gave up His life on the cross and returned to heaven, He did not leave us comfortless. He sent the Holy Spirit (John 14:17 NKJ) to help, empower, guide, go with, teach, and comfort us on our journey. After accepting Jesus Christ as Lord and Savior, the Holy Spirit becomes available and ready to go alongside us as a friend, to equip and enable us to walk in obedience. After acceptance, we now have the capability of understanding the Bible and living out this Christian walk. The Holy Spirit will be there every step of the way. It is solely up to us to heed or acknowledge His leading.

Satan

Now comes Satan (II Timothy 2:26 NKJ), who, along with his fallen angels, are God's archenemies. For a while longer, Satan holds the title as the Prince of this World, whereby he uses his position and power to tempt and mislead humanity. Satan's desire is to disrupt God's plan by influencing the lusts and temptations that are deeply embedded in our carnal

> Satan wants to influence the one power God has given to all humans, our ability to choose.

hearts and minds. Satan is the accuser of brethren, boldly standing up to God to tell Him how bad we are. Satan wants to influence the one power God has given to all humans, our ability to choose. Satan is not omnipresent; he cannot be in all places at the same time as God can. This may be one of the reasons why his attacks seem to come in waves, since he must split his focus between his many targets. Satan will cleverly use the setbacks, tragedies, and weights of life to tempt and mislead us into following his desires. Satan and his evil forces are always fighting against God's efforts to redeem humans.

The Flesh

Next, there is the flesh (Romans 7:5 NKJ). This is the conscious, emotional side of the human which has the propensity to sway man's ability to choose self-will over God's. Parts of the flesh have an insatiable thirst for riches, lusts, and pleasure. The flesh is stubborn and hates to be under authority. It is always striving to make the individual's wishes the center of attention. It approves unruly motives and tries to replace God's will with its own ideas.

The World

Lastly, there is the World (Romans 12:2 NKJ) and its views which must be addressed. Worldliness is the point of view and wishes of a society which in most cases derive from self and are opposed to Christian standards. Those of this world's view have a set of values and beliefs which shape their perspective, opinions, and then their actions.

Each of the above spirits can show up at any time. Don't let a lack of information about who's who in the Bible weaken and cause you to wander as it did me. Nevertheless, if you don't believe spiritual forces exist, then you're already being influenced. I hope my brief description helps you to recognize who is fighting for you and who is trying to deceive you.

Although my father was out of position in the home and sometimes negligent in his role of nurturing, God wasn't. He had preordained a divine plan for me to prosper. Yet, with each bad choice I made, I could have forfeited all that God had in store for me and so can you. It had been a few months since I almost drowned and God was still setting up unmerited moves.

While walking alongside the highway one afternoon, a small orange pickup truck pulled up beside me. Inside was a white man and a little boy. "Excuse me kid, my name is Larry Spivey, and this is my son Walker. Officer Omar Spivey is my brother. You're Bennie Powell's son, right?"

"Yes sir," I answered.

"How old are you?"

"I am almost nine, sir."

"Have you ever played baseball?"

"No sir."

"I am the Coach of my son's team, and we could use another player if you want to try it. Get on; we are headed to practice right now." In no way am I advocating getting into cars with strangers but for some unknown reason, I crossed that boundary that day!

Upon arriving at the baseball field where other kids were gathering, I noticed that most kids had on new spikes and gloves. Me, I had on a pair of old beat-up sneakers, and I didn't even own a glove.

"Hey, you guys gather up," shouted Coach.

First, he pointed out the group of volunteer coaches who were also dads. Then he introduced me to the players and told them to say their names one by one. Afterwards, Coach thoughtfully asked me what hand I threw the ball with, so I raised up my left.

He then reached down into his equipment bag and tossed me an old glove. "Now, all of you partner up and go warm up your arms."

After warm-ups, the Coach split us into groups, then led me to first base and started to give me basic instructions while the other players were working in the outfield. Even though I was left-handed, Coach systematically tried me in various positions including shortstop.

I had trouble with all aspects of the game, from catching, to the point of stopping a rolling ball on the ground. Everything was tricky for me. Although I did not throw with precision and smoothness, throwing the ball was my greatest asset by far, simply because I unexplainably threw harder than the other kids. By the time practice was over, things had loosened up and I was super excited. I still remember how Coach regularly stopped practicing to explain practical lessons, so we would be better equipped to manage those game-changing moments that lie ahead.

Coach was the first man I had ever encountered who took the time to explain consequential things to me. I cannot recall a time when our family or Dad sat down to talk about the six above-mentioned role players. Conversations about self-control and boundaries were also topics that got overlooked. This mode of abandonment was long in place before I was born and it all started with neglect. Sharing first-hand information could have prepared my brothers and I to better manage some of life's bitter moments which lay ahead.

Don't skip over the details about life and Godliness when it comes to your kids.

CHAPTER 4

Caught in a Pickle

His own iniquities entrap the wicked man,
and he is caught in the cords of his own sins.
—Proverbs 5:22 NKJ

In baseball, a rundown is also called a pickle. That is when a baserunner gets trapped between two opposing players who are trying to close the gap and tag out the baserunner before he advances to the next base or returns safely to the prior one. Every day, Satan and his imps want to catch, trick, trap, and pick us off before we advance in knowledge or come to understand God's purpose for our lives.

The belief that I controlled my own destiny and decision-making played right into Satan's trap. It was this type of foolish thinking that landed me in to some difficult situations I called "pickles."

While mom and dad worked, my grandmother or Big Momma as we called her was my caretaker. We spent a lot of days together; some good and some not so good. There were numerous occasions when I would catch Big Momma napping in dad's recliner and foolishly sneak into the kitchen to take one of her mouthwatering biscuits. She always knew I was the culprit because I was the only one home at the time of her discovery. I also remember her sending me outside to collect my own rod of correction from a bush before reluctantly spanking me and repeatedly saying mid-swing, "This hurts me more than it hurts you." Sorry Grandma, but I humbly disagree. Although I had felt the sting of her whippings, it still didn't break my spirit to go and take another biscuit the next time. Now here's the thing: I'm sure she would have given me a biscuit if I had only asked, but for some unexplained reason that thought never entered my mind. One of her day-to-day admonishments for me was, "Boy, one day, you're going to get yourself into some serious trouble."

After living what many would consider to be a full life, I can still recall the sadness I felt when Big Momma died. She was eighty-one. Since that was my first encounter with death, I had no previous experience about how I should react. I never got the chance to cordially say goodbye to her at her funeral because mom thought I was too young to go. Big Momma's death left a hole in my heart and many unanswered questions about the condition known as death. Death had silenced one of the most important voices in my life who was concerned about my actions.

Big Momma's death uncovered our family's shortcomings and immediately placed them on the critical list. Her presence had anchored the family in many ways. I do not know how she did it, but I had seen the sheer presence of her feeble little frame slowly sliding into the room and extinguishing Dad's temper before he had a chance to fully erupt. Death, whether in a child or an adult, can bring about complete devastation, especially if

> Death is one of Satan's most underrated strongholds because it seizes the dead and sometimes traps the living.

the deceased person was the one stabilizing the family. Death is one of Satan's most underrated strongholds because it seizes the dead and sometimes traps the living.

Without delay, our negative behavior (the flesh), and the subtleness of Satan infiltrated the lives of the rest of the family and began making an already somber mood worse. Eventually, Dad and Mom's fussing grew more intense while my brothers' appetite for mischief escalated. Regrettably, I was not exempt and followed suit by getting into more and more trouble myself. In short, things were continuing to come apart at the seams and Dad didn't have the spiritual awareness to stop it from unraveling. For the next few years, our family slipped more and more into a silent cycle between seclusion and disappointment. No one outside the family came to our rescue either because they didn't know about Dad's erratic behavior, or they just chose to mind their own business.

I will never know the depth of grief my dad was experiencing when our family lost Big Momma. Now as an adult, I can imagine that maybe part of his anger came from this second loss of a mother figure. His mother had died when he was just a boy, and now his respected mother-in-law was also gone. Not knowing how to process such pain could have been part of the reason Dad continued to detach from his wife and sons. Whatever the reasons, Dad wasn't able to control our family's decline.

Men, we must pay close attention to our actions, words, and promises. The deeds we commit in front of our sons as well as others will always leave an impression, especially when it pertains to them and their moms. We must consider consequential losses before we get caught within the rundowns of abuse, addiction, anger, and a lack of concern. My Dad's attention to work and play continued as normal, which did nothing to improve things at home with us boys. What and who we ignore to check on, talk to, or see about, we will eventually lose.

> What and who we ignore to check on, talk to, or see about, we will eventually lose.

Up to this point, I had done some ridiculous things. The silliest and dumbest had to be stealing candy while I had the money in my pocket to pay for what I had stolen. According to Proverbs 22:15, my behavior exposed a level of folly which is present in the heart of a child that must be supervised and then extinguished.

At the raw age of sixteen, some years after Big Momma's death, I heightened the offence from taking biscuits, to candy, and then to stealing money from a nearby business. After hearing about one of my friends being picked up and questioned, guilt and shame set in. Even though I felt I had gotten away with the theft, I kept quiet. Somehow Officer Spivey, my one-time baseball coach still came to the house—not as Coach but as a police officer with some questions for me. Without hesitation, mom invited him in. I honestly can't remember at what point during the questioning I broke, however, at some point, I inexplicably admitted guilt to taking the money. The stunned look on mom's face turned to shock and then tears as Officer Spivey stood me up, placed me under arrest, and walked me outside.

As he was placing me into the back seat of his patrol car, our cousin walked up and I could hear Mom uncontrollably crying and saying to her, "That's my baby he's putting in that car; that's my baby." Somehow, the pettiness of sneaking biscuits had evolved into a more serious pursuit.

No sooner than the door of the patrol car closed behind me, Mom's cries grew faint. Instead, the only voice and words I heard echoing in my ears were those of my grandmother saying, "Boy, one day you are going to get yourself into some serious trouble." The fulfillment of Big Momma's prophecy arrived with haste and snatched away my freedom.

As the patrol car inched away from the driveway, I looked back only to catch a glimpse of my cousin Barb hugging and consoling my devastated mother.

Sometimes, we think our quest for pleasure only affects us, but that is a lie from hell. Regardless of age, gender, or status, chasing after unpleasant desires can trap, emotionally exhaust, and hurt all the people who we're supposed to love and care about.

Next, Officer Spivey made a stop at Norman Park City Hall where we exited the car and proceeded inside. While inside, he made several phone calls while I sat in an adjacent chair across the room. We were there for what seemed like an hour before I was escorted back outside and transferred to another officer's car. It was at this point that I overheard my next destination, the Albany Detention Center. The ensuing forty-five-mile ride produced a level of anxiety like I had never felt before. I started to cry, and the farther away from home we drove, the more delirious I became. The officer tried to calm me down, but I was so flustered I could not pull it together. Recalling my mom's anguish as I was being taken away seemed to fuel my fear and anxiety.

Other than when Coach Spivey picked me up to go to baseball practices, this was my first time being in the backseat of a police car as a criminal.

As we drove up to the Juvenile Correctional Detention Center in Albany, Georgia, my bloodshot eyes traced the towering 15-foot chain-linked fence around the grounds. The Deputy parked, opened the car door, and asked me to step out. Next, he escorted me inside to the director's office where I was given a short orientation of the facility and an explanation of the zero tolerance rules. In juvenile detention everything was mandatory, beginning with a 6:25AM alarm to get ready for breakfast at

7:00AM. Everyone was given different assignments, from cleaning the bathrooms, mopping the floors, working in the kitchen, and even raking leaves around the grounds outside. There were daily counseling sessions where topics in education, vocational training, behavior, and reintegration were addressed.

After we left the director's office, an officer over the juvenile division led me down the hallway. The jingling of the officer's keys walking behind me only hastened the beating of my heart rate. Then unexpectedly, the rattling stopped.

"Stop right here, this is your room."

After flipping through his keys and opening the door, I walked inside the tiny room and the door was closed behind me. An eerie silence greeted me as I stood there scanning the room. A single twin bed with a small nightstand sat against the wall. Above the nightstand was a small light with a round intercom speaker protruding underneath from the wall. Sitting adjacent to it against the other wall was a small desk and chair. As soon as I sat on the edge of the bed, the tears started flowing again. Up to this point, I had only asked God for one thing; fix my stuttering. However, that did not stop me from desperately praying and pleading with Him for another chance. There is no way God intended for me or anyone to spend their life locked away like animals in a zoo. I thought about the freedom outside that I had forfeited away until I eventually fell asleep.

On the second day of lock-up, just two days shy of New Year's Day 1980, my group had to go outside and rake the grounds around the facility. A chore I had hated so much at home made me feel human again. As the work intensified and the time passed, the South Georgia winds brought a familiar sound to my ears. I heard cheers coming from a baseball field across the street which caused me to stop raking and momentarily look up. The applause of that crowd reminded me of the game I loved and the liberty I once possessed. As I returned to raking, my eyes filled once again with tears. Had I ruined my life?

When New Year's had come and gone, by the ninth day of my arrest, incarceration had gotten my attention in ways everyday admonishments had failed to deliver.

One area which had continuously made me a better pitcher in baseball avoided me now. In baseball, I had been able to evaluate my mistakes, assess why I had made them, and adjust so that I wouldn't make that same mistake again. For some reason, I had been unable to use this same strategy in life. I did not consider any of the errors, miscues, or consequences that had derailed my brothers and hounded my dad. I was making the same kinds of defective choices they had made, and now I was receiving the negative results of such choices. Opportunities had presented themselves offering me the chance to see, learn from their actions, and then walk away from mischief, but I didn't heed them. Why couldn't I do in life what I did in baseball?

Nevertheless, Big Momma's words still reverberated in my head. "One day, you're going to get into some serious trouble." My hard-headed posture in the streets had turned into soft putty while I was following directives on the inside. Years of youthful mischief and willful disobedience had culminated in my losing of my freedom. Now, the stupidity of my actions was about to come to a head.

Later that same afternoon, I was taken to the director's office once again, where I was informed that my court hearing was scheduled for the next morning. The anxiety and uncertainty of what was around the corner made it very difficult for me to sleep that night. I lay there envisioning court and what the judge's verdict may be.

Throughout the drive to the court hearing, I trembled with uncertainty. As I entered the courtroom through the side door, I noticed my mom with her head down and the aggravating look on Dad's face. Mom stuck beside us through thick and thin. I remember her coming to the aid of my brothers and myself on countless occasions. She was strong, quiet, and the one who took care of us the best way she knew how, with love and devotion. I believe we were the only reason she chose to stay in a physically abusive relationship. Dad, on the other hand, had his own false three-strike method of hanging with us, and after that, he was not coming to our rescue anymore. Believe me, my brothers and I had obviously exhausted his approach years ago. We were boys learning as we went.

Mom lifted her head just in time to see me come into the courtroom. The pain and sadness in her eyes melted into relief as she gleamed and whispered in an emulating gesture, "I love you."

Dad had been at work when I was arrested, so I'm certain he preplanned to have this day off early in honor of mom's appeal. This was the first and only time I recalled my father ever missing work.

Waiting for a superior court judge to cast judgement on your future is not a pleasant position to be in. Nonetheless, I was both grateful and embarrassed when Officer Spivey stood up before the judge and advocated on my behalf.

In the closing of my case, the judge leaned forward and sternly looked down at me and issued this warning. "Son, if you come back into my courtroom ever again, I am going to send you away for a very long time." He then released me to my parents. I clearly heard every word the judge spoke that day.

After some time had passed, I learned that Officer Spivey had not only gone to bat for me with the judge, he had also reached out to a juvenile counselor after my admission of guilt. With hopes of scaring me straight, he probed early in the process with the authorities not to just release me right back to my parents. This was the type of friend he was to the Powell family—not just a coach or policeman. The fear and humiliation of ten days in incarceration had caused a major shift in my attitude. Too bad it did not stir up or change my relationship with Dad. Was I blaming my father for my constant failures as a teenager and young adult? At that time yes, I was. However, that was not a true assessment; Dad was not to blame. Sure, I missed his involvement, input, and guidance, but at the end of the day, the choice to do wrong was my own. God has given us all the ability to choose right—we must then choose it.

Fathers, we must stop blaming ignorance, work, our past, and significant others for our shortcomings. I will be the first to tell you that letting your sons learn as they go is a mistaken strategy you don't want to make. Teach them before society does. Young men, we can turn bitterness and anger into positives by committing to being the best father, provider, and protector for those we have helped create. Fatherhood is one of the greatest positions we could ever undertake. Let God show you how to turn things around for the best.

CHAPTER 5

Turning Point

I will bring the blind by a way they did not know; I will lead them in paths that they have not known: I will make darkness light before them, and crooked places straight.

—Isaiah 42:16 NKJ

Life is comparable to a baseball game because the ending can never be determined by its start. As a starting pitcher, I remember games where I struggled to control the opposition's scoring in the earlier innings where they took the lead. However, as the game progressed, I settled in and finally found my groove. That momentum shift gave my team a chance to chip away at the score before ultimately retaking the lead and the victory. Fair-weathered fans hurled insults and negativity while I pitched to bring my team back. In the same way, society found it easy to hurl insults and negativity at my earlier struggles without the thought of me ever turning my life around.

I was thirty years of age when I heard a pastor declare that "experience is not the best teacher; someone else's experience is the best teacher." The lessons I should've gathered from my brothers while growing up eluded me and the ones they should've learned from me also went unnoticed. My brothers' momentary thrills almost cost them their freedom and in some cases, it nearly cost them their lives. Their negative choices and brushes with the law should have been all the proof I needed to stay clear of trouble. After what I had just gone through with incarceration, I no longer wanted to follow their pattern; but moral knowledge without the power to obey it can be quite frustrating.

After my release, it took only a few days for the people in my community to pick up a familiar chant they had thrown at my older brothers. Regretfully, my past actions provided them with the necessary energy and platform to voice their criticism. The words they used to shape me were, "You will never amount to anything." They had already condemned, sentenced, and prophesied my outcome as a loser before anyone saw what God had planned. (I would later learn that God had good plans for me and everyone else. See Jeremiah 29:11.) It is astounding the piercing things people will say and do when you're backed into a corner with nowhere to turn.

One mandatory rule we had while in lock up was that we must sit in daily consultation groups. It was during these meetings that the counselor repeatedly mentioned two fundamental principles which eventually walked out of detention with me.

"Take heed to your surroundings."

"Always be aware of who was within your circle."

Thank God, I learned somethings while on the inside that are still fundamental principles of my life today. The agony of being jailed had triggered positive changes within my heart, yet it was going to take time and effort for them to manifest outwardly in my behaviors. I started staying home more while turning my attention back to baseball.

After sitting out my junior year of high school baseball with an arm problem, I returned my senior year with an inexplicable drive. That 1981 season marked a turning point in my baseball journey. Before games, I regularly scanned the bleachers and surrounding area looking for family members. However, the whole time I was going through my metamorphosis, Satan was continuing his assault on my family by shooting burning arrows of busyness and self-interest into their lives. Not to mention, Dad was still being consumed by his work and pursuits. Nonetheless, their absence did not change the way I performed that season. I excelled so well at pitching; I received the team's most valuable pitcher award at the team banquet. Still, no member of the family showed up to support my accomplishments.

The next challenge in my life was just as startling and scary as juvenile hall. Graduation was just around the corner, and I had followed the wrong crowd in pursuing vain relationships, fun, and not a higher education. I had concluded twelve years of schooling only to approach graduation with no career goals in mind. In fact, even if a college recruiter would've shown me some interest, my overall state of mind wouldn't have allowed me to pursue college. This common adolescent mistake made life after high school all the more uncertain.

At this point in time, my brother Jimmy and his girlfriend had just moved into a house together. Benny Lee and Calvin came home at odd times of the night, if they came home at all. With no post-graduation plans in sight, what came next for me was not surprising. I watched television, stayed up late, slept half the day, and roamed the streets the rest of the time. This lazy cycle repeated itself for about two months until my brother Calvin walked in one day and impulsively started to lash out at me for not looking for work.

It took a little while, but I eventually found a job on a milk dairy farm. Farm work was a common occupation in the country. My main task was to feed and bring in about a hundred cows for milking. For this reason, I had to learn how to drive an old pickup truck to haul hay and other stuff around on the farm. Because of all the open pasture in which to steer and make mistakes, it was quite easy for me to learn how to drive. Sure, I ran the truck into a ditch a couple of times, but we easily pulled it out with the tractor. I worked on that milk dairy farm for about two months before Mr. Pace, the owner, took me off the farm to work in his grocery store.

In a small town like Norman Park, I am sure he knew of or heard of some of my past troubles. Nonetheless, he trusted me. I was now working as a stock-boy just a mile away from home. I kept this new job until one month shy of my eighteenth birthday.

When it came to decision-making, maturity did not come with age, so from time to time I hit a snag but nothing too serious.

Whether you're a teenager or an adult, Friday nights in Georgia meant high school football. It was easy to get a ride to the games, but since the school was 10 –11 miles away, if you wanted to stick around after the game, you had to figure out another way to get back home. Every time, just moments away from the game being over, I would then start thinking about how I'd get home. Whoever I hitched a ride with after the game would often determine where I ended up.

So, I quickly reviewed the places I could go for the best time. It was either the youth center, the American Legion, or the McDonalds parking lot. The most popular for the young Black crowd was the youth center. Next, there was the McDonald's parking lot for a mixture of both races but mostly whites. McDonald's was just like a scene out of *Happy Days* the TV show, where the kids just cruised around Arnold's. Then we had the Legion. This is where the older crowd fled for fun. Outside all three venues in the parking lot were the intoxicating, tempting lures of girls, marijuana, and alcohol.

I decided on going to the youth center with a group of friends, hoping to see Mel. Mel was a young lady with whom I had a secret infatuation. In school, I was a nervous lightweight when it came down to partying and girls. Therefore, I always had to put up a good front. After scoring a cup of rum and coke, I stuck around for a little while before deciding to move on. Next,

I caught a ride to the American Legion. The parking lot scene was buzzing with young and older Black people standing around or sitting atop their cars. Some had doors open while the bumping sounds of *Fantastic Voyage* by Lakeside were vibrating out of the speakers and into the air.

As soon as we exited the car, you could smell the marijuana in the air. I never saw who lit it up, but the next thing I knew, someone was passing it to me. I took a couple of big hits and passed the joint along. I did not even stick around for it to come back a second time. That hit mixed with the alcohol from earlier set off the spinning in my head like a slot machine twirling in Vegas. I could already feel the buzz creeping up. In some psychological way, smoking weed built my confidence. Remarkably, I did not stutter as much when I was high. The sensation after taking a hit removed my insecurities. Therefore, when I saw Mel, I got lost in the moment, which caused me to lose track of time. And as you might imagine, by the time I found a ride back to Norman Park, I had missed curfew by an hour.

Although I was still quite under the influence, I had the wherewith all to know that a fatherly storm was brewing on the horizon. So, before I exited the car, I mentally cleared my head and prepared myself for the worst. I slowly turned the doorknob only to find it locked. Next, I lightly knocked on the door. After a few seconds elapsed, Mom opened the door and said nothing. As luck would have it, Dad had gotten drunk and had gone to bed. Relieved, I hurried to the room, undressed, and got into bed.

The next morning Dad stuck his head through the curtain and shockingly told me not to leave the house. Without any more threats or drama, he had grounded me! That was very odd coming from Dad, but I decided to take it. Grounding was way better than having him go completely off on me.

About two hours after Dad left, my cousin appeared in the front yard calling my name. "Can you come with me to Ed's house to pick up the barrel grill for the cookout?"

I told him I was on punishment, yet he assured me we would come right back after the grill was loaded.

"I don't know man," I answered.

Once again, he promised, "We are coming right back."

Even though I had every intention of following Dad's orders, I said okay.

Once at Ed's house, we quickly loaded the grill and then went inside to get the meat. Just as my cousin exited the kitchen, Dad and Ed walked through the front door. I turned to explain myself. As Dad walked closer, I could see the venomous effects of alcohol in his eyes. Without saying a word and before I had a chance to utter anything, Dad backhand slapped me so hard that it turned my head around as I fell back onto the couch. As I lay disoriented and trying to shake off the effects of the slap, I realized that everyone else was frozen from obvious shock.

Without warning, I pushed myself up and dashed out the front door. The humiliation brought on by the slap was all the motivation I needed to start running. Within a minute or two into my heated dash, a recent conversation crossed my mind which caused me to slow down to a jog. Earlier in the week, Mr. Wallace, the manager of a semi-pro baseball team had offered me a job and a place to stay with two of the players if I joined his team. That slap, mixed with the invitation echoing in my head, supplied all the energy I needed to jog the rest of the way home.

Immediately after arriving home, I found Mr. Wallace's number and called to confirm his proposal again before accepting. I gave him consent to pick me up that same afternoon. I didn't know how it was going to play out or what I had just done. I just followed my emotions. The embarrassment of the slap consumed me as I tossed whatever I had for clothing into a duffle bag. I had about forty dollars and no experience at living on my own. Yet, that didn't stop me from getting ready. I had gone too far to turn around now. About two hours later, I heard Dad's car pull into the yard. Assuming it wasn't over yet, and that Dad was about to enter for round two, I quickly stuffed my packed bags inside the small closet.

Dad stormed into the house banging the walls with his masculinity as he sat down and started pressing in on me again. The louder he yelled, the more I bickered under my breath. He shouted threats, but once again, there was no apology, explanation, or personal reasoning for his actions. Dictatorship was one area where my dad's boldness stood tall.

As my anger emboldened me, I uttered, "One of these days, I'm going to leave."

"You are not going anywhere," he instinctively shouted.

I thought to myself, *I'm never going to allow you to knock me down again.*

After a few moments, everything settled down as Dad drifted off to sleep in front of the television. Honestly, I was stunned that no one from Ed's house came to check on my condition. When Mr. Wallace arrived a few hours later. I grabbed my things and without any hesitation, I calmly walked out the front door while Dad sat snoring in the chair. Not once did my emotions let me look back. During the drive, I got the impression while listening to Mr. Wallace that my two roomies, Joe, and Rod, were going to be excellent guardians. It sounded like an ideal setup.

After I calmed enough to consider my actions, I called Mom, and we talked at length about all that had transpired. She had no idea her baby had moved out. Not once did I consider her feelings or care about what Dad might say later.

Mom tried to cover for Dad. "You know how your father gets when he is drinking; he didn't mean any harm."

"I know I was wrong for leaving home Mom, but he slapped me in front of everyone. This is a good opportunity for me, and I am not going to miss it. My mind is made up, and I'm not coming back. I have a place to stay and a job delivering ice to convenience stores."

Mom didn't approve but in the length of the exchange she accepted my request. I finished the conversation with my mom by saying, "Trust me Mom, I will be okay."

At the end of the day, Rod and Joe stood in and helped build me up in neglected areas where society had mentally torn me down. Each did a first-rate job at keeping up with me. Most importantly, they seemed genuinely interested in my future and well-being.

Rod and Joe asked me about my life, my goals, and my plans to achieve them. I had no plans. They asked questions my father should have asked. All I wanted to know from Dad was whether he cared or not about me and my challenges. Why wasn't he available for my ball games on the weekends? I wanted to hear my dad say, "I love you, and I am here for you." There is a part of my mind that wanted to know why he never took the time to play, talk, or explain the pressures and pleasures of being a man.

Men, it's no longer a secret. If we're going to turn our sons around or help them with their challenges, we must start with availability, truth, and then support. Fellows, we must also pay attention to our circle of influence and friends. Do we have guys in our circle who will tell us when we're going the wrong way or about to do the wrong thing? Do the men we get advice from encourage or discourage us when needed?

That slap on the face from my father froze all who stood in the room that day. However, it set off a chain of events that pushed me right out the front door and onto a speedy road to adulthood.

CHAPTER 6

Silencing the Crowd

It is God's will that your honorable lives should silence those ignorant people who make foolish accusations against you.
—I Peter 2:15 NLT

Throughout my career, I've heard both the cheers and jeers of baseball fans. When I wasn't pitching up to their satisfaction, casual fans did not hesitate to yell out their disapproval. Each level I achieved, the better my focus and execution had to be to maintain. I learned how to adapt both to positive and negative chatter. There were incidents at which I had to shrug off racist remarks from other players and even umpires. Regrettably, I also had to deal with insincere teammates who wanted me to fail so they could take over my role. Unfortunately, that same level of inequity towards Black men still lives on in society today. As I aged, I realized how to take on a different mindset and method to keep moving forward. Most men will never get the opportunity to play in the major leagues, but they will get a chance to shine in the role of fatherhood. In this game, the stakes of winning and losing a son will be much higher.

It had been a little over a year and a half since I walked out of detention. A mental shift had taken place, but few noticed or acknowledged it, including Dad. Still, God's mercy was about to afford me the grace to reach another level while silencing most of my critics in the process.

On the first day of practice with the Hawks baseball team, something occurred that was mind-blowing. My thoughts took me back to the day I had to rake leaves during incarceration. I remember hearing the cheers coming from the people down the street at the ballpark. Astonishingly, that same baseball field would now be my new home park. This was a blessing I never saw coming. Standing on this side of the chalked lines felt much more civilized than being behind that chain-linked fence glistening off in the distance.

My very first opportunity to pitch at home resulted in my going the distance. I pitched a complete game which we easily won. As I exited the park that day, I couldn't help staring across and down the street in total awe. Walking behind and beside me were a few Hawk supporters building me up with congratulatory remarks. What was once applause for someone else had now morphed into cheers for me!

Each game I pitched thereafter slowly changed my destiny and further silenced the voices of my critics. Even my dad and I let the pressure of our last encounter blow over. We didn't exactly reconcile, but we did talk every now and then.

During my first few games, I left it all on the field as I put together a string of very impressive performances which had already earned me the prominence of an All-Star. Success not only silenced the naysayers in my life, but it also strengthened my self-confidence. It gave me the belief to proudly hold my head up high.

After the span of about six to seven games, our manager, Mr. Wallace, briefly spoke to me about one of his contacts. Some of the greatest opportunities we will ever obtain will come through availability and not just ability. My first invitation came from Coach Spivey along the highway that day as a young kid. Neither of us knew his roadside offer to play baseball would one day lead me to something greater.

Several weeks went by and without warning, I was approached again by Mr. Wallace and another man. The first words out of the man's mouth were, "That was a good game. My name is Tommy Mixon; I'm a scout for the Los Angeles Dodgers."

After pausing for a moment to let that sink in, he asked, "Have you ever considered pro ball?"

"Not really, I just go out and play."

After that pitiful answer, he asked a few more pertinent background questions which I honestly answered. As I stood there still confused as to what was happening, Mr. Mixon said, "I will be in touch in a few days." Next, we shook hands and he walked away. I didn't know what to make of that moment, so I kept it to myself. Little did I know that this short conversation was another opportunity I never saw coming.

After about five days, Mr. Mixon contacted me and to my amazement, he informed me that the Los Angeles Dodgers were interested in signing me to a minor league contract.

On May 17, 1983, I met Mr. Mixon at the Norman Park City Hall with my parents, Officer Spivey, and a local photographer from the *Moultrie Observer* to sign my first professional contract. God was once again rewriting a misstep of my past. He had already caused me to reestablish a connection with my father. Once, City Hall had been the setting where I was transferred from one police car to the other. Now, it was the backdrop to another unbelievable moment in my life. The Dodgers offered me three thousand dollars to sign and a one-way plane ticket to Bradenton, Florida, to play on the Dodgers rookie team. It did not matter what they offered me; I believe I would have signed for free. Regardless of what is going on in your life right now, it's not over until God says it's over. He can turn your life and situation around while silencing all who oppose you.

The good news of my signing spread like wildfire. A kid viewed by many as a failure was painfully slapped onto a path by his father. Now, I would be competing amongst the best in the baseball world. I was so naïve about professional baseball and its steps, I honestly thought I was going straight to Dodger stadium. I never knew there were levels to climb in the minor leagues.

The majority of guys hoping to make it to the majors spend years in rookie-ball, A-ball, double A, and triple A levels, and never make it to a big-league team. Since I was from Georgia, I knew of the Atlanta Braves, not any minor league teams leading to the Braves. However, my favorite team to watch was the Pittsburgh Pirates with Willie Stargell, Bill Madlock, John Candeleria, and Dave Parker.

At the conclusion of my very first season in professional baseball, the writers of the *Sporting News* selected me the "Star of Stars" award winner for my 1983 Rookie season. That award is the same as Most Valuable Player of the whole league. I finished that season with 8 wins and 2 losses and a 1.46 ERA. The talent and budding seed of potential which God had deposited in me before birth had sprouted into something special as I moved quickly through the minors. My 1984 Single A stop in Vero Beach, Florida, lasted about a month before I was promoted to AA San Antonio, Texas, where I finished with a 9-8 record. Just like in life, the game was getting tougher, but I was still processing and learning as I went.

In 1985, after another promotion, I opened in Albuquerque, New Mexico at the triple A level; just one step from the majors. I started that season with a perfect 9-0 won-loss record and an earned run average of 2.74.

Next up, Honolulu, Hawaii. It was my most anticipated trip of the season because I had never been to Hawaii. The only familiarities I had of Hawaii came from watching television shows like *Hawaii 5-O*, and a *Sanford and Son* episode. We were flying there to play the Pittsburgh Pirate's triple A club. Nonetheless, I was about to finally see the beaches of Honolulu for myself.

As luck would have it, I received a window seat from the traveling secretary. During most flights, I found it easy to sleep but my excitement wouldn't let me sleep on this one. The whole trip from Albuquerque via Los Angeles to Hawaii lasted a little over seven hours. As you can imagine, the view from the plane as we descended was breathtaking. Seeing the blue waters and white sand caused my heart to race with excitement.

Upon arrival, I grabbed my bags and loaded them onto the team bus. Soon after, the bus came to a stop at the team hotel, we started unloading our bags and equipment. Next, one of the players behind me said, "Hey Powell, Coach is calling for you at the front desk." I stopped what I was doing and headed inside.

As I approached, Coach had a puzzling look on his face. "Gather up your bags; you have another flight to catch."

"Where am I going?"

"You just got traded."

"I-did! To whom?"

Now, with a big smile, "To the big leagues," he replied.

"You're joking!"

"Nope, you just got called up to the major leagues. A reservation has already been made for you to join the team in St. Louis for Sunday's day game. Congratulations, you've certainly earned it."

With both disbelief and eagerness, I shook Coach's and some of my teammates' hands. And just like that my enthusiasm for Hawaii took a backseat to something even more spectacular—I was headed to the majors!

After making an emotional decision less than two years ago to leave home, I was now just ten hours away from joining the Los Angeles Dodgers for a series against the St. Louis Cardinals. This was a trip I had never dreamed of taking.

When I arrived in St. Louis on Sunday morning, I had instructions to go straight to the team hotel. I'm sure the cab driver saw the smile on my face that stretched from ear-to-ear. Words cannot describe how I was feeling. My insides hadn't stopped celebrating since Coach broke the news. As the taxi approached downtown, I could see the Gateway Arch off in the distance. I thought my excitement could not go up anymore until I caught a glimpse of St. Louis' Busch stadium. The stadium was located just across the street from the team hotel. After checking in, I hurried to the room for a shower and to phone my parents to share the good news. I knew they were proud when I first signed and given a ticket to the rookie team, but I also sensed they were just as oblivious to my call-up as I was to the idea of reaching the big leagues. There were no pre-written scripts for parents to follow when you're the first from your family or area to reach a level such as this.

After hanging up, I eagerly went downstairs and headed out through the side doors for the stadium. I had to pass through some early autograph seekers who were waiting for star players like Valenzuela, Hershiser, Welch, Sax, Yeager, and Guerrero to come out. To my surprise, some in the group knew of my promotion and asked for my autograph.

After a little rerouting from outside stadium attendees, I was finally inside and just a few steps away from the entrance to the visitors' clubhouse.

As I pulled open the door, I felt both an indescribable nervousness and an amazing sense of accomplishment. The clubhouse attendant greeted me and led me to my locker. A number 48 jersey and uniform were already hanging inside. The difference between a big-league clubhouse and a minor league locker room was night and day. In the minors, the clubhouses were small and filled with tiny lockers. Clubhouse attendees had snacks like peanut butter and jelly, chili, cold cut sandwiches, and if we were lucky, dessert after the games. On the contrary, a big-league clubhouse had all the gratifications of a superstore. The center aisle was completely stocked with coffee, donuts, bagels, cream cheese, bubble gum, sunflower seeds, potato chips, and cookies. The table next to it was garnished with fruit, veggies, and all kinds of sandwich meats to enjoy. The refrigerator was stocked with juices and sodas. There were also couches, tables, and televisions for our comfort and enjoyment.

As I patiently sat at my locker, team manager Tommy Lasorda and the traveling secretary came through the door and surprisingly welcomed me as they made their way to Tommy's office. As other players trickled in, each one echoed the same sentiment, "Congratulation's rookie."

After putting on my practice jersey, I walked out to the dugout and just stared over the stands as stadium employees made their way throughout the seats. What a view from this perspective. As I sat watching them, I heard another voice, "Congratulations Powell. Keep doing what got you here; it's the same game." It was one of the other coaches coming in from running the stands for workout.

Coach was correct about it being the same game, but what he failed to point out was the magnitude of the new plateau. Everything about the majors was major—from the size of the locker to the amount of available free snacks, to the caliber of players, to the amount of the paycheck, to the expectations, and more. Up here, I wasn't going to get away with throwing mislocated fastballs and the hanging curves which I consistently got away with in the minors.

It had already been an unforgettable day but as I watched from the bullpen as the game unfolded, my mind suddenly turned to when I would get my clance. The game had moved into the top of the seventh inning when the phone rang. Next, I heard "Powell get ready." After grabbing a cup of water and chugging it down, I started warming up. Then a few minutes later the phone rang again, and coach said those words that still make me beam with joy, "You're in kid." The previous pitcher gave me just enough time to get ready when he went back out to start the bottom of the seventh.

When the commentator announced my name, I trotted out to what seemed like a chorus of 36,313 boo's. After all, this was the home of the Cardinals.

By the time I arrived at the front of the mound and took the baseball from the manager, my mouth was bone dry. As the manager walked away, the catcher and I got our signs together, and then he turned and trotted back to home plate. Next, I walked down the backside of the mound and mustered up as much saliva as I could to wet my throat. I then bent over, picked up the white rosin bag and firmly squeezed it to dry my sweating palm. Afterwards, I nervously walked up onto the mound, dug in my cleats, and threw my first of eight warm-up pitches. By the end of my first inning in the majors, I had robotically followed all the signs my catcher put down and actively pitched a scoreless inning. At the end of two debut innings, I walked two, I threw one wild pitch, and surrendered one run. I gave up my first hit to Terry Pendleton and threw my first major league strikeout to Tito Landrum. A journey that started back on a dusty field in Norman Park, Georgia, had led this stuttering little boy to the glitz and glamour of the major leagues. The road had led from the Moultrie Recreation Department playing against VFW and Harper McCall to now pitching to Ozzie Smith and the Cardinals.

Soon after the game, our team departed for the airport and then we were off to Pittsburgh for a series against the Pirates. It wasn't until we checked into the hotel in Pittsburg that I called my parents with news of my performance in St. Louis and shared that the team would be coming to Atlanta soon.

Men, it's not over until God says it's over. No matter how life starts, God can help you go the distance and win with your sons if you would just give Him a chance. Don't let past shames shade or cloud expectations for your sons. Stop listening to and singing the you'll-never-be-anything anthem over your boys.

Throughout the earlier levels of life, I had placed disgrace onto my family via personal failures which were hard to escape. Yet, God mercifully positioned people along the way somehow to help me find my way. A son who has been troubled still has gifts into which he can grow. His gifts can shine even though he's been in trouble in the past. "A man's gift makes room for him" Proverbs 18:16a.

As men, we must grow and change as our sons develop. Fathers, we cannot use the same approach nor mentally operate as our dads used to back in the day. We must be aware of the ever-changing laws, system of beliefs, and moral values with which our sons are bombarded on a daily basis. Know that a huge future awaits once you become watchful and patient to take the necessary steps. "For I know the thoughts that I think toward you, says the LORD, thoughts of peace and not of evil, to give you a future and a hope" Jeremiah 29:11.

Bear in mind, when God assigned man the tasks of leading, protecting, and providing for the family, He also provided him with the means to fulfill the assignment. Like going through the different levels to get to the major leagues, be aware of making progress in steps. Celebrate your sons' advancements along the way. We can block out the debilitating criticism of societal crowds by repositioning ourselves to applaud subtle victories in and with our sons.

As a father, I have felt some of what my parents must have experienced in worry, but not to the degree they agonized with me. Everything I needed to capture and silence negative thoughts started with me knowing my identity in Christ Jesus. This force alone is also all I needed to silence the discouraging voices I heard concerning my father and those sent to devalue my sons' efforts while growing.

By the time my minor league career ended, I had pitched 976 innings with 60 wins and 45 losses. My Earned Run Average was a satisfying 3.55. I had racked up a professional career which had silenced a lot of critics. To God be the glory.

CHAPTER 7

Never Saw it Coming

Just as you cannot understand the path of the wind or the mystery of a tiny baby growing in its mother's womb, so you cannot understand the activity of God, who does all things.
—Ecclesiastes 11:5 NLT

In 2022 and according to Matrix AMM, the average exit velocity of a baseball leaving the bat in the Major leagues was 91.8 and 92.8 miles per hour. However, the highest exit speed came off of the bat of Pittsburg Pirate's Rookie shortstop, O'Neil Cruz clocked at 122.4 miles per hour. Picture the horrifying force behind a ball moving at that rate and colliding with the head of a pitcher who never saw it coming. Over the years, the results of such collisions have varied from concussions, mouths wired shut, loss of memory, broken jaws, to seizures. Recovering from a traumatic injury can be challenging. Some players have rallied back after devastating injuries, while others were never the same. This is where the cliche "I never saw it coming" comes to mind and sets the stage for another impactful turn in my life.

A little over two months after my promotion, our team boarded the team's chartered plane for a flight to Atlanta. This would be my first-time seeing mom and dad since the call-up.

As I reclined in my seat and closed my eyes, an earlier assertion from one of my coaches resurfaced in my head. "Keep doing what got you here, it's the same game." Coach's words were spot-on. Yet, there were several other off-the-field details he and others had failed to point out about the Majors.

Regardless of playing time or status, many wonderful and mesmerizing things came wrapped inside the big league package. Chartered planes, limousines, classy restaurants, custom clothing, jewelry, and five-star hotels were all at our fingertips. Additionally, nightclubs, exclusive parties, drugs, and girls also caught our interest. I'm not mentioning these things to glamorize or condemn the profession; I simply want to reveal the whole playing field.

As I moved higher, I learned through errors and miscalculations that there were different temptations waiting for me at each new level I achieved. Unfortunately, my past experiences with neglect and stuttering had not prepared me for all the attention I would receive in the Majors. To the contrary, those experiences had groomed me to shun the spotlight that regularly shined on pro athletes.

> there were different temptations waiting for me at each new level I achieved.

By the time our five-game series against the Atlanta Braves had come to an end, the attention was on me when I walked away with a few emotional firsts that turned out to be gratifying. On Monday, the very first night, September 9, 1985, I pitched two shutout innings of relief to earn my first professional save in front of family and friends who had made the 197-mile trip up from Norman Park.

After exiting the clubhouse, a group of young boys crowded around me to get autographs. As I signed one of the boy's baseball programs, I remember hearing one say, "I wish I was you, Mr. Powell." Wanting to walk in someone else's shoes without knowing their plight or road travelled is a common mistake we all make." Little boys only want the moments of praise, while men recognize that there had to be some hardships that preceded the triumph. If only that kid knew the painful path I undertook, maybe he would've changed his request.

For a moment I glanced up only to catch a glimpse of different people congratulating and hugging my parents. Individuals from my hometown who had branded me a loser while growing up were some of the same folks embracing them now. Mom kept wiping tears from her eyes while Dad stood tall and proud with a big smile on his face. At that moment, I saw God wiping away some of the childhood embarrassments which I had placed on my family. He was now replacing them with a liberating crown of honor and glory.

After what I had just done on the field, the family and I went out to celebrate with dinner. Next, I headed back to the hotel because I had to play in a doubleheader the next day.

As soon as I laid down, I noticed the red light blinking on the base of the phone signifying some type of message. I called the hotel operator and to my surprise, the message was from Gwyn, a girl I had briefly chatted with while signing autographs before the game. I remember her well because her youthful beauty is what got my attention in the first place.

Without hesitation, I wrote down the number she had left and right away started to dial. Because of the hour, it turned out to be a brief but interesting exchange of personal interests and usual first-time inquiries. Nevertheless, our dialogue did lead to a pregame meet up at a sandwich shop the next day seeing as she worked near the hotel.

I couldn't have written a better script for myself because later that afternoon after lunch, I pitched four strong innings, while allowing just one run for my first major league win. To accomplish this second feat while more family and friends watched on television back home in Norman Park made it all the more special.

Since my brothers were still in town, after the double header, we headed to a nearby restaurant for one last chance to hang out. When my brothers went back to their hotel, Gwyn and I met up knowing that I was leaving right after Thursday's game. It was a very pleasant get-together filled with flirtation and laughter. Be that as it may, we reluctantly ended Tuesday night and made plans to hook up again the next night. We even talked a little more on the phone after she made it home. That next and last night proved that physical attraction and idleness should never be placed in the same room with the buildup of chemistry and inexperience. At some point during the night, we irresponsibly crossed sexual boundaries for the first time. Although I made some rash promises that night, we only talked briefly before that last game.

Given that communication was not one of my strongest attributes, I only spoke to her a couple of times after I got back to Los Angeles. No sooner than the season was finished, I was on the road driving back home to Georgia.in my recently purchased brand-new White, Chevy IROC-Z.

After my first week home, I managed to call Gwyn before planning a trip up to Atlanta. It was simply me making light of time since I was leaving for winter ball in the Dominican Republic in a couple of weeks. There we were on several occasions, two young people fascinated again by outward looks, playing with fire and the forbidden fruits of passion staring back at us. In my mind, the distance between Los Angeles, Norman Park, and Atlanta combined with my no girlfriend mentality kept the relationship from advancing any further and in the friend's zone.

Anyway, three months came and went, and my first stint in the Dominican Republic had just passed. At this point, the 1986 spring training season was upon me and I was super excited about the opportunity which lay ahead. Although I was only home from Dominican a day or so, I did manage to see Gwyn before leaving again.

Since I lived in Georgia, I was one of only two players granted permission to drive to big-league camp. Therefore, I left for Vero Beach, Florida, two days before I had to report.

Upon arrival, I realized I was a twenty-two-year-old rookie surrounded by veteran players ranging upwards to 38 years of age. They were a very distinct group of older men, some of whom had excelled on the field at an extremely high level. Some had wives and some were single with lots of experience both on and off the field.

Case in point: one Friday afternoon mid spring training, a couple of teammates invited me to a club after practice. They asked me to drive. The evening started off with a happy hour stop before heading into a nightclub. Over the course of the evening, both teammates took off with some girls they had met, leaving me to drive back alone, foolishly under the influence. With the music entertaining me, the ride back to the facility was relatively smooth. As I entered the first of the last two turns traveling at about 20-25 miles per hour, my focus and thoughts shifted from the road to changing the song on radio. Suddenly, a sharp light flashed across my eyes as my head bounced off the steering wheel. The front right bumper of my car had glanced off of the guardrail and crashed into a light-pole. I had failed to straighten up out of the curve. Panicked and dazed, I quickly exited the car and started walking.

I had managed to drive about twenty miles back before wrecking. Camp was only a quarter mile down the road. As I entered, walking undetected past the security office at Dodger town, I had the wherewithal to go straight to our trainer's room and start knocking. He opened the door and gasped at my bloody face and shirt. Next, he pulled me in, rushed off, and grabbed a towel to press against the cut in the middle of my forehead. Perceiving that the gash wasn't as bad as first anticipated, he settled. Next, he got dressed and drove me to the hospital. I needed six stitches to close up the gash.

Eventually, management and the police were advised of the incident which happened about 12:30 AM. Since I was back at camp, the police mercifully did not perform a breath analyzer or issue me a DUI citation.

Promptly the next day, I was demoted from the big-league side back down to the minor league side as a form of punishment. I was only on the minor side for a little while before pitching my way back to the big-league side. Fortunately, I was good enough to break camp—get back on the big-league roster—before the team headed back to Los Angeles. After my IROC-Z was repaired, I had it shipped to me.

While that 1986 season had its moments, some intimate decisions I made prior to the season back at home began to show themselves. We make casual choices all the time and yet the outcome differs. Driving under the influence was definitely wrong and a bad choice. So many innocent lives have been destroyed by this careless act in judgement. Similar to it but not equal, entering into sexual situations without conscience, care, or commitment to outcome is also reckless and dangerous.

Throughout the span of the season, I had started receiving news from Gwyn that I was going to be a father. From the outset, I instinctively questioned motive and timing since I thought we used all the right protections to cover the bases. Disappointingly, the initial news of pregnancy did not come with the celebratory reaction it deserved. I was 22 years old and the immaturity showed in my actions. At season's end, I did not willfully communicate or see her in person.

At the time of the birth, I was playing in my second winter-ball season in the Dominican Republic. It wasn't until I returned home, heard from my mother, and saw the baby pictures that I knew Dennis Jr. was my son. His strong facial features and resemblance could not be denied. Nevertheless, I still allowed the uncommitted long-distance relationship with his mom to block me from getting close to him in the earlier years. In fact, the pregnancy split up our friendship in ways I never anticipated before his birth. I used mistrust as an excuse but in actuality, I was scared and didn't know what the hell I was doing.

Regrettably, the one who had no choice in the matter was also the one who would be most devastated later by my actions: my son. When parents can't get it together, the child is the one who is affected the most. Many sons face the burden of having to deal with the complex emotions that come with being the child of a single parent. These sons must adjust to getting picked up from one house and dropped off at another. They wonder, "Why can't I see my dad," and "Why can't I stay longer?" They must constantly try to acclimate to the different moods of each household. This kind of existence can be traumatic and life-altering for him.

As I was writing this chapter, I asked another man who had grown up without his father if he could ask his estranged dad one question, what would it be? He said, I would ask him, "How could he leave and continue to walk away while I was still crying "Daddy and calling for him?" This is a question so many men need to come back and answer. "Dad, why did you honestly walk away or deny me for so long?"

As I sit and reflect back to that time, the whole situation was something I never anticipated. I had blindly ushered in the same curse of abandonment to my son's generation as my father did to mine and his dad did to him. I just accepted and carried out the disillusioned role of fatherhood under a different excuse and name.

There are still a lot of men out there who have never recovered from the surprising and impacting news of their first child. Faultfinding scars of fear and pride never rewarded them with the courage to apologize or to express an explanation for running away.

My girlfriend, Brenda, came into the picture when my son was a baby, but she did not physically meet or see Dennis Jr. until he was about four. Once she met him, she made sure I stayed verbally connected to him by phone but sometimes even that was challenging for his mom and me knowing that I never gave the relationship between her and I a chance. After Brenda and my relationship evolved into marriage, we started traveling back to Georgia together. Each trip we would stop in Atlanta and pick up Dennis Jr. before continuing to see his grandmother for a few days. As he aged, he still had every right to feel abandoned because I lived in California and only saw him when I visited Georgia.

Although I supported him financially, I neglected my physical obligations to him. I was not there to lead and guide him. Making sure he had everything he needed in the early and later stages of his life was admirable, but what my son needed most was my time and attention. I was not there to correct his mistakes or demonstrate how a healthy father-son relationship should look. I was a professional baseball player who never came around to play catch or teach him about sports. Disappointingly, I was too immature to address the fracture, stress, and hurt that I caused his mom and him. At that juncture in life, I had no idea what came with the day-to-day responsibilities of being a father, much less a co-parent.

Once Dennis Jr. was in his teens, Gwyn did open up the door for him to start coming to California to visit me from time to time. Over the years, his mom had done a remarkable job getting him through unforeseen hardships the best way she knew how. I know it wasn't easy. Still, he had made his way through high school and was now in college. A few years after starting college, we received news from his mom that he had dropped out. My wife was quick to suggest that my son come live with us so we could get him back in school. I quickly agreed.

It started off well for us but as you might imagine, what he was feeling on the inside soon surfaced verbally and manifested on the outside. We kept trying to bond emotionally; however, house rules, curfew, and resentment got in the way. I was fighting to gain his approval, but years of pent-up disappointments and bottled-up emotions prevented him and me from making real progress. Again, the relationship broke down and became too hot for either of us to control. So, we had to go our separate ways. My son was actually traveling the same lonesome emotional path as I had travelled except, he did not have an impending job, or two awaiting adults to guide him as I encountered.

The separation between myself and my son was a battle and recovery which had to be fought and won with God's spirit.

I didn't know how, I didn't know when, I just knew that after things had escalated to that point, all I could do was to let go, pray, and place the broken pieces of our relationship in God's healing hands. I can't even tell you how this faceoff came to be, but it was an unplanned spirit-led moment which opened the door for a heart-to-heart sit-down between the three of us—the third person in the room was the Holy Spirit.

My son wanted to know if he was the reason his mom and I never got together. I answered "no" and explained how I let anger, fear, immaturity, and ignorance cause me to neglect my time with him. I could relate to his bitterness and piercing questions because although I had a father in the house, his absence also filled me with some of the same anger and emotions my son now held. I truthfully admitted to erring in my fatherly responsibilities. I explained how the relationship with his mom just didn't work out. I did not have any premeditated answers; however, I did have a box of receipts to show my efforts over the years. From birth to the present, my agent kept every payment of child support, daycare visits, babysitters, monies for Christmas, birthday gifts, and whatever else Gwyn needed to care for him. He and I sat there looking through everything, crying and letting our tears wash away critical and damaging remarks that had filled his head and mine with assumptions. Voices that told him he was unloved, fatherless, and an accident were slowly being purged. Once again, the Spirit of God intervened on my behalf in the form of my son accepting my apology and forgiveness. Overall, the sit-down helped us both to take a step forward in healing and to steer our relationship back onto the right path.

As I was writing this chapter, I called Dennis Jr. to get his consent to tell our story. I intentionally put this chapter in the middle of the book because a son growing up and making it without his father's input for an extended period is the heart of my story and testimony. Despite it happening so many years ago, I started to weep as I relived some of the memories and my actions. I was being reminded of just how much pain a mistake in judgement has on both the neglected son and the father's conscience.

There are fathers that long for time with their sons and I was no exception. God gave me the honor of getting my first Major-league save and win in front of my family. Years later, even though I did not see it coming, God blessed me with the chance to win my first son back through open honesty and being there for him.

Many fathers today have made the same reckless decision as I had done by entering into a sexual situation without conscience. Whether we think all is safe because of protection or not, there will be a consequence to our action. Whether it is pregnancy or maybe just a deeper sense of attachment from the girl, we have a responsibility to act with care, concern, and commitment if the former proves true and you are the father. So, don't let distance, a disagreement with the child's mother, or a new relationship stop you from getting close to your son.

Eventually, peace with Gwyn was restored and the devastating fractures my son and I suffered healed beautifully. Today, my son is standing over his home as protector and provider for his own family because I took my position, faced my mistakes, and stood up as the head of my home. This act of authenticity gave God the opportunity to put the shattered pieces of our lives back together. To see and know that Dennis Jr. is succeeding despite my negligence reveals just how much God loves him and so do I. For God Himself said in Hebrews 13:5, "I will never leave you nor forsake you." He has kept His promise.

Men, regardless of how fractured or damaged your relationship is with your son, God can reset the broken places. All you have to do is give Him a chance to shape you into the man you were meant to be. Then, we can cast off that disgraceful badge of being a "dead-beat dad" and embrace the privilege and honor of being a father. The game isn't over until God says it's over.

CHAPTER 8

Playing Out Of Control

A person without self-control is like a city
with broken-down walls.
—Proverbs 25:28 NLT

I had risen to a level in professional sports that thousands of prominent players had failed to reach, the Majors. I was getting paid to play a game I loved and would have played for free. The baseball field was a place where I had regularly excelled. Whenever tragedy struck off the field, I was able to put it aside while on the diamond. The field was a sanctuary to me, a place where I replaced pain with peace. Unfortunately, growing concerns about fatherhood, family matters, and faults cannot always be concealed or laid aside.

As the next season moved into the latter stages, I kept receiving disturbing news from Norman Park about this hard-hitting newcomer who had established quite a reputation in the streets. It was this revolutionary drug called Crack. Crack cocaine was a cheap, easily manufactured drug that exploded onto the scene in the early 80s leaving a path of destruction, not only in Georgia but all around the country. Crack instantly ripped apart families, marriages, and lives. This drug crossed all socioeconomic boundaries leaving most of its sufferers in already disadvantaged communities.

According to a 1984-1989 Harvard University study by Gerhard, the homicide rate doubled for Black males between the ages of 14-24. Black communities experienced a 20-100% increase in weapons arrests. People both young and old, male and female, were giving their control over to crack. They were burglarizing, assaulting, and doing sexual deeds just to get money for a date with this drug. According to Michelle Anderson, author of *The New Jim Crow* (2010), "Nothing has contributed more to the systematic mass incarceration of people of color in the United States than the War on Drugs. Two of the contributing factors were that men of color chose and could acquire the cheaper crack cocaine a lot easier than its counterpart, the more expensive powder cocaine.

At any rate, Mom kept hearing and reading stories in the newspaper about local crimes reaching an all-time high which naturally made her worry about my safety. As a result, she simply asked that I phone home after the season instead of trying to come home.

Without delay and against Mom's wishes, I still made and carried out my plans to hit the road for Georgia on the first Thursday after the season ended. Given that I was in no rush, the trip was a road trip filled with random pauses and mouthwatering food breaks in Arizona, Texas, Louisiana, and Florida.

At about one o'clock PM on Sunday afternoon, I passed the Moultrie, Georgia city limit sign. I was almost home—just another fifteen miles. However, before anyone knew of my arrival, I decided to drive through parts of Moultrie before continuing on to Norman Park. Places where I once partied, laughed, and ate were gone or dilapidated. Streets and parks that were once filled with action and activities were now ghostly. At that moment, I visibly sensed why Mom felt the way she did about my home-coming. The old stomping grounds as I knew them had changed their overall appeal. Instead of growing, they had deteriorated.

Before crack cocaine had ever arrived, the lives of many had already been weakened by a lack of fatherly attention. What crack revealed was how untrained we were as a generation to stand and face this powerful drug.

Once at home, I wanted to spend my first couple of days with Mom. However, as news of my arrival spread, we seemed to always have visitors knocking at the door. Each day turned into a small social get-together with food and family. As the time and days passed, I did manage to visit a few old elementary and high school teachers who had influenced my life. These were teachers who encouraged me through stuttering episodes and many other educational challenges I faced. The happiness on their faces as I entered their classes was well worth each visit. Each granted me the space to speak to their classes about the importance of education, the Drug Abuse Resistance Education program and my journey.

Irrespective of all the excitement regarding me, I still noticed how Dad was chasing his own personal desires after work while my brothers were yet languishing in their daily pleasures. I say that because although they were older than me, two of them still lived at home.

Continuing through life under the debilitating shadows of abandonment will not equip a father with the strength or discernment needed to restore health to his sons. As a father, I came to realize that the first step to change was acknowledging that I needed help.

Providing that little had advanced in the form of after-hours nightlife, I drove to Albany, Georgia on Friday to see some of my old Hawk teammates. Then on Saturday, I decided to party at the Legion in Moultrie. Before heading out, I picked up my cousin and we were off. On the way, we stopped, and I bought us a bottle of Cognac to carry inside.

By the time we arrived a short line had formed to enter the club. The atmosphere was electric. Schoolmates who recognized me were showing adulations from all sides. We entered through a pat down search and we were in. Somehow, my name made its way inside the club before I did because an unexpected shout-out from the club disc jockey welcomed me over the public address system. After that, I was instantly hurled into celebrity mode. That same big-league prestige I encountered in Hollywood had accompanied me back home. With each flicker of attention, a subtle weakness started to surface. In the blink of an eye, I had handed over control of my evening to the limelight and liquor. What eventually began in the club ended with me getting a room across town and inviting a small group over for an after party. The next morning, I got up, checked out of the room around ten, and ate breakfast before heading back to Mom's.

As I entered the house, Benny Lee, my oldest brother, promptly met me. One of the people crack cocaine had influenced was my oldest brother although I did not know to what degree.

"Hey Dent," Benny Lee queried, "can I borrow your car to go pick up my girlfriend from Omega? I really want you to meet her."

From day one of my arrival home, my oldest brother never let up his plea to drive my IROC-Z. My response had always been an echoing, "No!" Yet, I looked him up and down and felt he would never do anything to jeopardize our relationship or my car.

So, my response was, "Okay, please be careful and hurry back."

About an hour elapsed when my cousin Jean rushed through the front door and said, "Come and go with me, Benny Lee has wrecked your car." Since I was leaving on Tuesday, I thought she was trying to lure me to a going-away celebration, so I didn't rush.

"Give me a minute," I said.

As soon as I got into her car, she sped off in complete silence. We couldn't have driven more than five miles and as we came around the curve, my heart shuddered from the sight of blue flashing lights. As we got closer, I saw my car resting in a ditch on a large concrete sewer pipe. The front spoiler-kit and axle had been snatched completely underneath the car. A crowd had already formed.

"Where's my brother?" I frantically asked.

A random bystander answered. "When we pulled over this is what we saw. There was no one else here."

I scurried around looking for answers. Then, my brother's suspected whereabouts came over the two-way radio of one of the officers standing next to me. "We have a male suspect lying in a ditch off Highway 319 North, fitting the description of someone who has been in an accident."

Quickly, my cousin and I got back in the car and began to follow an officer back towards home. As we topped the hill, we saw the lights of another police car already parked in front of Mom's house. I quickly exited the car and rushed over to find my brother lying in the ditch, squirming and in pain. An officer was poking slightly around his rib area and at his legs.

When Benny Lee saw me, he immediately started apologizing. "Dent, I'm so sorry about your car."

My insides shutdown momentarily under the strain of not screaming, *"What have you done?"* Instead, I calmly said, "Don't worry about the car, I can always get another car. How are you doing?"

"My side hurts," he replied.

"Lie still so the officer can check you out."

Although only about an hour-or-so had elapsed, my brother looked as though he had been partying all night. He reeked of alcohol and the glassy, bloodshot gaze in his eyes told me he had also been smoking crack. The girlfriend's excuse to use my car seemed to have been a lie. About fifteen more minutes passed before an ambulance arrived.

Straightaway the paramedics started their assessment and bandaged Benny Lee up. Next, as a precaution, he was transported to the hospital before being taken into custody for drunk driving and leaving the scene of the accident. We had his bail posted as soon as permitted.

At the conclusion of their investigation, an officer gave me an eyewitness account of what had happened. "While speeding around the curve, Benny Lee lost control of the car and rammed into a sewer pipe. The witness hurried inside his home to call 911 and report the accident. However, before he could get back to the scene, your brother had climbed out of the car, limped away, and hitched a ride with a passerby. Whoever picked him up must have simply dropped him off in front of your neighbor's house. He obviously tried to make his way down into the yard but fell and a person walking by saw him in the ditch."

Benny Lee suffered a couple of broken ribs, a badly sprained knee, and some head lacerations, but nothing life-threatening.

I thought to myself, *"What type of person would pick up an obviously wounded hitchhiker from an accident and then drop him off without addressing his injuries?"*

Then it hit me. As men, we do this every time we pick up a conversation with another man who is showing noticeable signs of anger, addiction, anxiety, or abuse. Yet, we end any talks and drop him off without ever mentioning his mental state or affairs because we think it's not our business.

Deep down, I honestly believed my brother would've never betrayed my trust. However, we both failed that day by handing over control to someone or something else. My mistake in judgment and willingness to let him drive my car shifted my power into his hands, in the same way he lost control the moment he went under the influence of drugs and alcohol. The drugs were now in control and not my brother.

After this, slowly, day by day, the apprehensions about fatherhood and my brother's actions, coupled with my mother's concerns for her sons began to take control of my mind.

Yes, my brothers and I had been neglected along the way. Declining character traits in my brothers and I had started to surface and yes there should have been some blame. However, we had no reason to keep blaming Dad for our failures. We were in our 20s and 30s and needed to stop pulling the "blame Dad" card. We were the ones guilty of yielding to self-will, pressures, and daily temptations.

Looking back on that time when I returned home from pro ball, I was just as vulnerable to alcohol as those relinquishing their will to crack cocaine.

With this thought in mind, something that started at about age nine or ten from involuntary sips of beer, had in the long run evolved just like the biscuits I once stole from Big Momma's kitchen.

The weekend for the adults usually started on a Friday in the yard between our house and the neighbors. During these gatherings, alcohol was easily accessible. Anyone who gave us kids a drop of beer, wine, or liquor thinking that it couldn't hurt was wrong. Whether it was an uncle, aunt, brother, or neighbor, those sneaky little nips of alcohol were the gateway to attraction and a larger appetite. What is more, when Dads drank, cursed, or constantly acted out in front of their sons, it's more than likely one or all of the sons watching would copy one or all their actions. It is a harsh reality, that much of what children see, they mimic and given the chance, they will take it into their adulthood.

In my naïve state, being back home in a nice car, with money, and a title continued to reveal that and other areas of weaknesses. We all needed help, but we never sought it.

Back on the field, plenty of men from various races had passed through my life, most if not all had supported me in one way or another from the dugout. Nonetheless, it was alarming that off the field, the only voice calling the shots in my ears was the voice of mischief. Sadly, pride still had me fooled into thinking I had everything under control.

Unlike the paramedics who temporarily bandaged up my brother's wounds after the accident, Jesus is the Doctor who heals every pain we suffer in life. All we need to do, men, is obey and let the Holy Spirit take full control of our hearts through submission. I did not learn about the role, work, and power of the Holy Spirit until years later. I needed an accountability partner, a Friend (Holy Spirit) to help me establish boundaries. God has given us all an inborn capacity to know Who He is (Romans 1:19-20). However, having moral insight about righteousness doesn't benefit us if we don't have the spiritual power to obey it. Although God was present throughout my battles, it was years later before I truly invited Jesus Christ into my heart.

CHAPTER 9

Living on the Edge

Can a man take fire in his bosom and his clothes not be burned?
Can one walk on hot coals, and his feet not be seared?
—Proverbs 6:27, 28 NKJ

An edgy baserunner is one of the leading disruptions to a pitcher who is simply trying to do his job and get the batter out. As long as the runner stays on the base, he is protected. However, the moment he moves away from the base, he is no longer safe. Over my career, I've picked-off my share of anxious baserunners who had drifted too far off the base. By the same token, a Dad places himself in the same position as an aggressive baserunner when he continues to insistently move towards activities which lead him away from his duties at home. Whether it's with worldly pursuits, work, or worry, we run the risk of being caught off guard while our sons carelessly wander around in life.

Men, we must wake up to the importance of our role in our sons' lives. While there's nothing wrong with being aggressive when it comes to getting ahead in life, as a dad, we must move and stop seeing ourselves as just baserunners and start seeing ourselves as our sons' Coach for life. We must take the position to oversee and warn our sons about the regretful repercussions of losing focus and chasing ill-advised pastimes. The life changing lessons we've learned on our trip around the bases to adulthood, whether good or bad, can go a long way in encouraging them to be focused, resilient, and more disciplined as they grow to be men.

Prior to his passing, I heard Tel-evangelist Billy Graham preach a well-known slogan in 1987 which lots of people have recited over the years. He entitled the message, "Just Say No." For a man to "just say no" to the tempting distractions of life, he'll need help from the Holy Spirit. Dr. Graham's words stirred my thoughts emotionally, but they did not wake me up to take action. In Luke 24:49, when Jesus went back to heaven, He promised to send us back a Comforter. It was evident by my erratic decisions at times, I had not yet tapped into or submitted my will to the power of the Holy Spirit and was trying to face life on my own. I was truly still living on the edge.

After the car incident with Benny Lee was resolved, I flew back to California. As the plane was descending into Los Angeles International Airport, my eyes locked in on the shimmering skyline lights glistening downtown. Just as those bright lights outperformed the fading lights of the suburbs off in the distance, life in the Majors quickly rushed in to outshine everything else going on in my life, no matter how important any other thing may have been.

Although Hollywood is considered a gateway to stardom, there were also a lot of other opportunities for letdown. With trendy names like City of Angels, Tinsel-town, and La-La Land to describe it, I didn't have to look hard for action in Southern California because on any given night action found me.

As my abilities took me higher, public appeal exposed other areas in my character which still hadn't being established. What little I understood about dating emanated from what I had come to discover through trial and error.

Nevertheless, I remember the first time my teammate Kenny took me to this popular restaurant and nightclub on Sunset Boulevard called Carlos and Charlies. After he and I ate downstairs, we proceeded upstairs to a nightclub called El Privado's. This venue was a hot spot for seeing some of Hollywood's finest stars, popular musicians, and athletes such as us.

After we ordered a drink from the bartender, Kenny surprisingly called over a lady friend and introduced me. This was the first time I ever saw Brenda. She was beautiful and very stylish. Since I didn't like to dance, trying to strike up a conversation over loud music made things a little awkward. Therefore, she rejoined her friends. Still, I continued to study her moves while taking notice of her fun-loving personality. She did not draw attention to herself like some of the other women I had come across. There was something incredibly special about her. Before the night ended, I did manage to get her number, where she worked, and a hug.

Even though I was in a light-hearted relationship seeing someone else, I kept visualizing Brenda's face. After the initial phone call, it did not take me long to seek out her place of business. There were several instances when I impulsively drove to Pasadena just to see and say hello to her. After about a month, I peaceably broke-off ties to the other relationship. My every intention was to develop a better relationship with Brenda.

However, two months passed and before I could form that solid bond with Brenda, I left for Winter baseball. A few weeks in, I got traded to a new team, the Seattle Mariners. Just like that, my Dodger days were over. Next stop, Seattle, Washington. In an attempt to keep a connection, I flew Brenda out to Seattle for a short visit. About three days in, my immature actions and single-minded mentality went on display. The intentions of my trip failed as I followed some of my teammates to a nightclub leaving Brenda alone in the apartment for hours. My irresponsible behavior proved to be a deal-breaker. By the time I got back, Brenda had left. She had called one of my friends for a ride to the airport, thereby ending the relationship. She did not accept any of my calls or speak to me for a long time after that episode and who could blame her?

At the beginning of the season, my preconceived notion was to permanently stay in Seattle. However, once I experienced the daily rainy, cold, and icy weather from my balcony, I wanted no more and headed back to Cali. Anyway, that weather ended any debate in my mind; California was now going to be home.

Over the next year and before I had a chance to reunite with Brenda, I found myself scratching through the pricks and thorns of several other ill-advised relationships.

One afternoon while driving towards downtown Los Angeles, I hit a traffic jam on the 10 freeway which caused me to change my route. As I made my way onto Wilshire Blvd, I saw this attractive young lady crossing in front of me at the traffic light. I honked, then she turned and gently waved back. That little gesture made me pull over. Like a gentleman, I exited the car and introduced myself. She told me her name was Jackie. Next, I mentioned being in a rush to meet my agent for lunch and asked for her number. She asked about my agent. I told her I was a former Dodger baseball player now playing in Seattle. Mentioning being a Major leaguer made it easy for me to get her phone number and I was back on the road.

Later that night through conversation, Jackie revealed how she had traveled from Detroit to Hollywood with hopes of breaking into the movie industry. From the outset, she tried everything to establish a relationship but I was now content on going solo. I was not prepared nor ready to be in a committed relationship. I just wanted to chill out in my apartment and play the field. Still, whatever I needed, she did it; from picking up food, dropping off my clothes at the cleaners, to coming by late night. Since she had a roommate, we usually got together at my place. However, on one occasion, I stopped by her apartment to surprise her. After seeing her silver mustang parked out front, I went ahead and rang the doorbell. It took about a minute for someone to answer. As the door opened, my nose was immediately greeted by the odorous combination of potpourri-air freshener and marijuana. After taking a step inside, I gave her a hug, made my way over to the couch, and sat down. Jackie came straight out and told me she enjoyed smoking a little weed to relax after a long day at work. She assumed I would not want to be around drugs since I was a professional athlete. She was mistaken; it didn't bother me so long as I wasn't participating.

My stress relief of choice was found in a glass of Cognac brandy with two cubes of ice. Jackie was still courteous about smoking around me; she always asked. However, the subtleness of Satan slowly used her sweet words and past memories to ease me into taking a hit. I took a decent sized puff, inhaled, held it, and then let it out. Here it come—that sensation of floating off into la-la land, just like back in the Legion parking lot in Georgia. Once again, marijuana took my guileless personality to a more heightened sensation both as a pick-me-up and an aphrodisiac. That infrequent hit turned into one, big mood setting puff each time we got together. Yes, one big hit did it for me. It made her want to get up and go, but it turned me into a romancer who just wanted to lay around. Unfortunately, it was those types of unbridled and impulsive moments which kept me living on the edge.

As I look back over my life, whether in season or out of season, how to manage idleness proved to be an area I consistently struggled to control.

As I started resisting the urge to keep smoking and just chill out, the less I saw of Jackie. Like a puff of smoke, she faded and so did that relationship.

Sadly, a few weeks after Jackie, I strolled right into the mesmerizing clutches of another resentful situation because I was not practicing what I was preaching. I had spoken to students both in Georgia and California about the Drug Abuse Resistance Education program. These appearances focused on "saying no" to drinking and drugs. The mistake I kept making came from selfish, adolescent urges mixed with the intoxicating effects of alcohol and idleness. Sure I was older in age, and working professionally at a high level in life, but sadly, my lack of knowledge and aptitude in consistent decision making was being developed as I went.

With that being said, enter Rita. I didn't know it at the start, but Rita unfortunately had similar traits as Jackie. She usually came by my apartment since I preferred it that way. The odd thing about her visits was how she made a habit of staying just a couple of hours and then leaving. Her explanation was that she needed to get back home to her grandmother. Since I had met her grandmother before, there was no reason for me not to believe her. In fact, this come and go arrangement was something I enjoyed.

Fast forward to the day of her birthday. I told Rita that we could do whatever she wanted for her big day. Until now, we had always met at my place. That night, she wanted me to come over to her place. To liven up the festivities, I brought an open schedule, some wings, pizza, and a small bottle of booze. I arrived at her grandma's house around 8:00 pm. After she answered, I immediately greeted her with a kiss and a small gift. Rita seemed a little lethargic as she led me past her grandmother's room and upstairs to her loft-style bedroom. I assumed this was in an attempt not to wake her grandmother. Incense candles were burning, a musical track was softly coming out of the television screen, and movies sat atop the video recorder.

Right away, I made a couple of drinks and started munching on the pizza while she grabbed plates from downstairs. As we sat on the foot of her bed "sipping our dranks", I kept eating. She barely touched any food. About twenty-five minutes in, I asked to use the restroom. She pointed me its direction. As soon as I returned, I noticed she had already refilled my glass; and was now sitting comfortably on the loveseat with a slight gleam in her eye. As I sat down, she handed me my drink and gave me a kiss. "Tonight, I want you to party with me."

With confusion in my voice, I answered, "I am partying with you."

She then reached down next to the loveseat and pulled up this small, lidless cigar box with some paraphernalia inside. My first thought was marijuana. Without flinching, she flicked the lighter and placed it at the end of a glass pipe which was already prepared. Boy, did I miss the mark! It was a piece of Crack. As she took a puff, I took a sip from my drink. After closing her eyes and holding it in for a moment, she exhaled. Without any hesitancy, she began putting another small piece of Crack in the pipe before shoving it in my direction.

"Take a little puff," she said "and hold it in."

As perplexing as this may sound, I did not shy away or take the offer as an insult. In fact, I felt a strange craving to find out what my oldest brother Benny Lee was fighting at home. I thought to myself, *What harm would one hit do?* As I foolishly reached for it, I chuckled and walked right into another inexcusable trap.

I took a hit, leaned back into the chair, closed my eyes, and experienced a rush like never before. I literally felt my heart thumping against the wall of my chest. As soon as I mellowed out, I immediately and unexpectedly felt an intense urge to take another hit but I refused. Hearing my heartbeat scared the hell out of me, but it did not make me run. I resisted most of the night to take another hit on the pipe and returned to just drinking. Whenever the urge came back I withstood; however, before the night was over I yielded and took another hit. Since I couldn't sleep, I stayed up until the early hours before leaving.

In James 1:14, the Bible says, "Each one is tempted when he is drawn away by his own desires and enticed." Again, I had no one to blame for this stupid decision but myself. The only thing sin did was use a lack of knowledge to cunningly entice the lust I already had inside. It was up to me to say no, except I did not have the spiritual power or wisdom of the Holy Spirit to say no to the subtleness of the moment.

I senselessly told myself, I could stop anytime I wanted since I walked away after two hits, but days later, I went back over to her place looking to recapture that first feeling. The mental urge to take a hit got stronger each time I did it. I literally felt an inner conscience part of me fighting against the enticement of my own sinful actions.

R. Zaccharias quoted, "Sin will take you farther than you want to go, keep you longer than you want to stay, and cost you more than you want pay."

As I look back, I now understand what Paul was implying in Romans 7:15 where he states, "For what I am doing, I do not understand. For what I will to do, that I do not practice; but what I hate, that I do." For me, a sense of paranoia accompanied each hit. I felt like someone was always watching or lurking outside.

Anytime an evil spirit comes across the naive, it looks for ways to capture and control the simpleminded person's innocence. I was the prey. Internally, I was stuck in this lying cycle of thinking all was under control. I now know from John 8:44, that Satan is the father of lies. Satan is not to blame for all I encountered since he is not omnipresent, but he and his imps do look for ways to sabotage the trained and untrained.

In fact, I was now four weeks into this relationship and the fight was real. I was too blind to see what was taking place. Had I paid more attention to Rita, I would have noticed some of the same behaviors my brother Benny Lee displayed just a year prior. She would hastily leave at odd times while I chilled. Her attire and physical qualities changed. We had given in to a drug that had taken most of the romance away and could've killed us in a single hit.

Knowing that another season of Winter ball was looming, I began to put up the fight of my life to get clean. I had to go back to work! I tried to resist, and I should have just walked away but I didn't. When Rita asked for money, I began to say no. This method worked sometimes because she couldn't buy the Crack, but my refusal didn't always stop her from acquiring the drugs, then I'd fold and take another hit.

Although I was trying to quit for my imminent return to baseball, Rita became shifty and more annoyed around me. The conduct she revealed when I started to refuse caught my attention. Rita was an addict. She stooped to whatever means necessary to get high. After staying over and subsequently falling asleep one night, I quickly concluded she had reached the bottom. She had gone through my pockets while I slept. When I awoke, I noticed the placement of my pants was odd. Then I detected some money missing. Just like the biscuits with Big Momma, I know for sure she took it because there was no one else around to blame. I then asked her to show me the bracelet I bought for her birthday; she couldn't provide it.

The mercy and all-powerful grace of God mixed with the hurt of her betrayal was the intervention I needed to supernaturally walk out and instantly be delivered from the enticing grips of Crack and Rita. Because she stole from me and never attempted to apologize or explain, we spoke only two other times over the next year.

At this point, I understood a little better the uphill battle my brother had been facing. It did not matter whether he was weak or strong. This drug carries no weaknesses and harbors no prejudices. It greets anyone who welcomes and gives it attention.

Over the years, I discovered from the testimony of a recovered addict, that a crack user will never experience that first rush of adrenalin and excitement again. That is the trickiness of crack; it makes you chase something you will never feel again. Each time we put a bigger rock of cocaine onto the pipe to capture that first sensation, we risked heart stoppage. He went on to say that his pursuits to recapture that first feeling landed him in jail. The drug pushed him to living on the edge. He stole from his family, girlfriend, strangers. He committed burglaries and even brutally assaulted people to get money. In addition to losing his family and job, on several occasions, he nearly lost the precious gift of life.

> That is the trickiness of crack; it makes you chase something you will never feel again.

Equally, Rita voluntarily sacrificed her dignity and our relationship to keep searching for that initial thrill. A once beautiful, smart, intelligent young woman fell prey to this deadly drug.

This is the persuasiveness of drugs and alcohol. They have the potential to temporarily ease our pain while on the flip side they can cause us to forget our identity and worth. Many have turned to doctor-prescribed pills, legalized marijuana, or even food with the hopes of finding temporary relief from the hardships of life. Yet, once the gateway swings open, many have lost their way to alcohol, opioids, and performance enhancing drugs, and have been swallowed up by the all-inclusive side effects of addiction and or death.

After five weeks of being pulled deeper into this fight, God graced me with the strength to walk away.

It is meaningless to have both the moral and spiritual knowledge about something dangerous if you do not have the power to say no to it. Satan's greatest area of assault is being sure that we never couple our moral and spiritual knowledge with the power of the Holy Spirit. In other words, the enemy does not care what you know, as long as you refuse to submit to God's power to help you live out what you know. I knew using drugs and alcohol were wrong and dangerous, but I had no power to resist their influence since I had not yielded to allow the power of the Holy Spirit to reign in my life.

> Satan's greatest area of assault is being sure that we never couple our moral and spiritual knowledge with the power of the Holy Spirit.

Therefore, we as fathers must share our experiences with our sons in the hope that they will not get picked off by drugs, women, alcohol, and Satan. The above incidents wouldn't be the last time I got knocked down, but it would be the last time I touched cocaine. Thank God, that snare was broken because I was walking on the edge of life experimenting and learning valuable lessons on the fly.

CHAPTER 10

Knocked Down but Not Out

When you pass through the waters, I will be with you;
and through the rivers, they shall not overflow you.
When you walk through the fire, you shall not be burned...
—Isaiah 43:2 NKJ

Purpose pitches are intentionally thrown to fluster the batter and make him uncomfortable. They would also set up my next pitch. When a batter is on a hot streak, I would deliberately throw a series of purpose pitches, either low and in to make him move his feet, or up and in to raise his eye level. This approach reminded me of my second season with the Seattle Mariners when life reversed my role and made this pitcher the batter because a series of events flustered me, made me uncomfortable, and turned my world upside down.

On April 3, 1989, we had just arrived in Oakland, California, for a three-game series against the Oakland A's. Shortly after entering my hotel room, the phone unexpectedly rang. Thinking it was one of my teammates, I rushed to answer it.

To my surprise, it was my cousin Barb.

"Dent, I am so sorry to tell you this, but Calvin and his son Dominic were killed in a car accident." I went down as if someone was choking me. My mind went into disbelief mode as I tried to absorb the news. Like a blistering fastball buzzing up and around my head, my brother Calvin, and my three-year-old nephew flashed in front of my eyes. As my sobs intensified, tears came streaming down my cheeks.

"How are mom and dad?" I asked faintly,

"Your mom is taking it hardest, but we're here."

"Let them know that as soon as I can get a flight, I'm on my way home."

I immediately called the team's traveling secretary to tell him of my family emergency. To my surprise, he already knew. A family member reaching out to the front office had informed them of this tragic news. With the team's corporate connections, I was on a flight to Albany, Georgia, in under three hours, although the entire trip would take about seven hours. I wouldn't get there until the next day, but the flight gave me a lot of time to reflect on my brother. From Atlanta, I took a smaller plane to Albany and then a car the rest of the way.

Before arriving, I told myself I had to be strong for Mom. The only thing I could do when I saw her was to hug her. As we sat crying together, the phone rang. It was Brenda, my soon-to-be wife. She was checking to see if I had made it home safely. After hearing that I made it and that I would be okay, she cordially hung up.

As the days passed, Mom went into a debilitating state of holding photographs of Calvin while staring at pieces of his belongings. Like most homes, pictures of the family hung all over the living room walls. I wanted to take her out of this environment, but I would never ask her to leave home to find peace and comfort.

On top of all that had already happened, a sweeping curve was coming around the corner.

A curveball is an amazingly effective pitch, especially if thrown after a purposely placed fastball to set it up. The curveball has a buckling, freezing effect on the batter because the batter thinks the ball is about to hit him. Yet, at the last moment, the rotational spin of the ball causes it to break away from the batter and back toward home plate.

About eight months before Calvin's death, my oldest brother Benny Lee tried to commit strong-arm robbery of a convenience store clerk. Strong-arm suggests he was not armed; he used force to overpower the clerk. The strong pull of crack cocaine and a lack of money pushed him to commit this desperate act. The courts sentenced him to a thirteen-month stint in the Georgia State Penitentiary. Everyone felt his punishment was a merciful sentence since he had been in trouble before. We held out hope that prison would serve as a detoxifying place for him to get free from his cocaine addiction. Although he still had a few months remaining on his sentence, the State of Georgia graciously allowed him a Compassionate Pass to attend the funeral.

Benny Lee arrived at the house a half-hour before we were to leave for the church on the day of the funeral. Before leaving, the escorting officers checked the rooms of the house and allowed him to change into more proper clothing. Still, he had to ride in an unmarked patrol car. However, at the funeral, we all sat in the front row while the officers blended into the crowd.

As you can imagine, people stood around the two distinctly different-sized caskets, giving remarks about my departed brother and nephew. Mom's agonizing whimpers filled the front pews with the kind of sighs a grieving mother could utter. I say that because, across the aisle, Dominic's mom was experiencing the same grief. I do not know whether Benny Lee's presence made matters better or worse, nevertheless, I was thankful he was here. Pleasant thoughts of Calvin filled my mind, but nothing could suppress the hurt. While sitting there, I was not thinking of myself, my dad, or my other brothers. I just wanted to stop Mom's pain. It was tough seeing Mom and Dad burying one of their sons while the other one went back to prison.

I was thankful and relieved to see the officers that escorted my brother standing off to the side in civilian clothes. One officer stationed himself at the back door of the church while the other stood posted at the front entrance. They were respectful in giving my brother space to grieve. At the same time, it was hurtful and distracting to think about my family's failings that seemed to be being displayed so publicly.

At the end of the ceremony and burial, the officers gave my brother about twenty minutes to say his goodbyes before taking him home to change. What's more, I was scheduled to leave in the morning to rejoin the team in Anaheim for a game against the California Angels. Life had knocked us down again, but we were not out.

The night before my redeye departure, the mood in the house was still somber. Dad and I embraced before I left. He tried to comfort me by saying they would be okay. The flight back to Anaheim the next morning went smoothly. On April 9th, 1989, I landed in time to make it to our 1:05pm game. That same afternoon, I pitched 3 1/3 scoreless innings of relief. After retiring my last batter, I lifted my face to the sky and raised my arms while reminiscing about Calvin and Dominic as I walked off the field. The hand and grace of God were what carried me through that game and still guides me to this day.

Things were not going so badly over the next few months. Through my next 20 1/3 innings, I only allowed three earned runs before inconsistency started to creep in. Benny Lee got out of prison, and Brenda and I got married. A new year and decade were approaching and things were looking up.

Then on January 20, 1990, during the off season, just eight months after Calvin's funeral, without warning, life unleashed a vicious slider. A slider has the same effect and look of a curveball; the only difference is the movements are sharper and swifter.

The phone rang, so I leaned over and picked it up. "Dent."

"I'm so sorry to always be the bearer of bad news." It was my cousin Barb again.

A momentary silence stood uncomfortably between us. "What's going on?"

My facial expression changed, so Brenda moved closer.

"Benny Lee, Jimmy, and Lemon were killed in an automobile accident." These were my other two brothers and a friend from the neighborhood.

Shock and disbelief immediately replaced the calm that had been in the room. "Barb, please don't tell me that, we just buried Calvin. What happened?"

"A car turned right into their path as they were coming back from Omega."

"Where are Mom and Dad? Let them know I'm on the way."

"We're looking after them, Dent. Get here as fast as you can."

As I sat with my mouth open failing to process the news, Brenda asked, "What's the matter?"

Tears came streaming down my face as I tried to get the words out, but nothing came. Then, I let out this painful screech that only God could comprehend. "Benny Lee and Jimmy were killed in a car accident."

Brenda sat down beside me and started to rub my back. Her touch seemed to pull the agonizing news more to the surface. Instinctively, I stood up and walked away while crying as Brenda began to pray aloud. It had only been 43 days since Brenda and I had gotten married, and Life was flexing its ugly muscles once again.

Since leaving prison, Benny Lee had been improving. He had made great strides in his life and was taking a turn for the better. He had started dating a girl who genuinely had his best interest at heart. She had even persuaded him to start going to church from time to time. Now his life had been cut short at only thirty-three years of age. Three brothers, a nephew, and a close friend of the family had been struck down in just eight months.

I could still hear Brenda passionately praying in the next room. "Lord, give Dennis and the family the strength they need to deal with these tragedies. Be with them as they go through yet another challenge. Lord, let them feel Your presence encamping about them."

Brenda knew God and the power that was in His son, Jesus. Me, I knew of God but I hadn't fully established a personal relationship with Jesus Christ. This season of heartache was one of the very reasons why I believed God positioned Brenda in my life. She had access to the only Source who could help safely guide me through these catastrophes. Brenda gave me the inspiration and courage to move forward in the face of opposition.

Calvin's death, a reversal of luck on the mound, and getting married all happening around the same time were challenging enough, but now I had to turn right around and face another traumatic and disruptive "pitch" which left my head spinning. I made reservations to go home. Brenda and I decided that I would leave the following day and then she would join me a few days later. This trip proved to be harder than the first. Again, I wanted to be strong for my mother's sake. What caring son would not want to ease the hurt and anguish his mom was experiencing?

My cousin Barb picked me up at the airport and filled me in on what was going on. She gave me details of the accident and let me in on the mood around the house. As she gave me the latest news, I could not hold back the tears. Afterwards, a deep silence overcame us as we drove home. The closer we got to home the more depressed I felt. When we arrived, parked cars were lined up on both sides of the road.

As I walked into the packed front room, family and friends parted a way for me to go directly to Mom. My heart broke once again as I caught a glimpse of her. She was holding pictures of all my brothers and crying as if she had just received the news. I knelt by the recliner and Mom pulled my head into her chest and squeezed it tight.

"My babies, my babies," she bawled.

"It's going to be all right." That was the only lame thing I could think to say.

"I know it will, but it doesn't stop the pain."

"I know it doesn't, Mom."

My first task was to convince Mom to lie down, and to do that, I had Barb thank everyone for coming. Slowly and respectfully, people made their way outside where others had gathered in the yard.

Once again, an unpleasant cloud hovered over the entire family. We needed strength that only God could provide.

Each of my brothers' accidents happened on the same highway just a few miles from home. Calvin's irresponsible mistake of passing a car while approaching a hill happened three miles on the Southside, while the other one involving Benny Lee and Jimmy was about six miles away on the Northside. Incidentally, Benny Lee's fatal accident was just three miles from where he had earlier wrecked my car.

On the day of the funeral, family, friends, and co-workers packed into Morning Grove Baptist Church to pay their respects. I was determined to be strong for Mom, but once again I sat and stared at two closed caskets. My father's face was set like a piece of granite. An occasional tear would trickle down his cheek as he stared. Death has a way of cutting off all your strength. I didn't want Mom or Dad to have to endure a long service, so I asked the pastor to keep things short and respectful.

Brenda was the angel we all needed that day. Thank God for her faithful witness. She seemed to know when to sit in silent prayer and when to speak. Mom somehow drew strength from her company. I am not even sure Brenda knew it, but the sheer presence of God within her was comforting the entire family while God kept us afloat.

Despite everything that was happening, I still did not make the final connection with God. Medicine prescribed by a doctor doesn't work properly if it's not taken in its entirety or according to directions. Although my sorrow ran deep, God's word did not comfort me as it should have because my profession of faith was only with my lips and not with my heart. At that time in my life, I talked the talk of a Christian, but I did not walk the walk of one. In moments of adversity, it was easy for me to follow my own path rather than the one God prescribed. We were all hurting from these tragedies, yet Dad held his emotion in. He did not cry, scream, or show any weakness. Maybe that was his way of showing strength. Still, as leader and head of the house, Dad needed to stand over home—comforting Mom more than ever.

Knowing what I know now as a father of four, I cannot fathom the unbearable grief and weight that was on my father's shoulders at that moment. Just the thought of having to bury three of my sons and a grandson within an eight-month period would have destroyed me. Don't get me wrong, I do have an understanding of my dad's silence at this time.

About a year or so after my brothers' funerals, I called my father just to talk. I wanted to relay a message about being a father. Sure, there were a lot of opportunities he had missed with his sons. He left out rules, talks, and many pertinent pieces of information which would have helped us mature. Yet, once we got to an age of accountability, we were the ones responsible for our actions. Things we knew and learned from Mom, teachers, other parents and experiences were readily accessible whenever we needed them. All we had to do was choose good.

As I thanked Dad for all the curfews, he started to weep and slowly break. The more I talked to him about his efforts, the more he released his guilt. I had personally forgiven him a long time ago, but I had never told him that these accidents were not his fault. I also wanted him to hear all the good I was enjoying as a father who was married and doing well because of his courage to stay with us and do the best he could for his family. Life had knocked Dad down repeatedly with news that seemed to always come in high and tight, but God began to raise him up with my words of affirmation. I thanked him for his years of fatherly labor and reminded him that we were still victorious.

I knew the curse had been broken that day, but I also knew it would take the power of God to restore his dignity. By the time I hung up, I felt my father's breakthrough was at hand. He had broken free of his cell of pain and regret.

CHAPTER 11

Breakthrough

Open my eyes, that I may see wondrous things from Your law.
—Psalms 119:18 NKJ

During my time in the majors, players did not have the computerized capability of reviewing their in-game performance from the bench. Nowadays, a player can promptly return to the bench and study his most recent undertakings on an iPad or laptop from the dugout. Sometimes this examination is all the analysis he needs to discover the issue hindering his performance. What a breakthrough!

While I'm on the subject of advancement and breakthrough, mental health and wellness were not as seriously considered as they are today. The emotional glitches in a person's personality and productivity were rarely discussed following tragic events in their lives. I remember having to pitch and carry on as normal the morning after burying my brother Calvin and his son. However, if I had been pitching today, mental health counseling would have been one of the first courses of action prescribed. This mode of caring is what I needed during this season of adversity, however, the only probing I got to reprocess life's latest tragedies was the question, "How are you doing? Are you okay?" Why ask a person who has lost three brothers, a nephew, and a close friend in less than a year if he is fine? It should have been obvious that I was going through a lot, because in general, when people lose loved ones, those grieving are not okay.

Case in point, I didn't have a chance to step away, rewind, and review all that had transpired. So, I continued to grope blindly through life.

Consistency on the field had always been an area of strength for me but shortly after those deaths from 1989 through 1991, that all changed. At times I went out and pitched well, but then in the games that followed, I was awful.

As dependability on the mound continued to lessen, seclusion, and self-prescribed drinking increased to numb the lingering memories which stayed in my mind. The notion to ask for help never crossed my mind. Since I had leaned on my cleverness as a teenager and young adult to manage many of life's earlier predicaments, I pridefully accepted the misrepresentation that I could handle anything. Unfortunately, the effects of those deaths—the pain and sorrow—were insidiously eating away at my effectiveness at an inconceivable rate. Nevertheless, pride still made me believe *I will eventually get through this.*

Sadly, there are many men who hold the same I-will-eventually-get-through-this belief when it comes to dealing with adversity. Male pride is a deceptive condition men yield to which starts small but grows as a silent killer like a cancer. One reason is, men are fixers by nature and to their own downfall, they try to resolve everything by themselves. Regardless of whether you are a father or not, men have taken on a lot of adversity and buried plenty of emotional stress over the years. So, I don't care how strong you are mentally or physically, there will be times when you must stop, step away from the action, and review your mental state. With that being said, don't go at it alone. Allow someone who is accountable and trustworthy to come alongside and be a sounding board.

After a subpar two months into the season, the Seattle Mariners released me and placed me on waivers. In layman's terms, my services were no longer needed. Seeing as this was the first time I had ever been released by a club, the dismissal just added to my emotional insecurity.

Within a few days, the Milwaukee Brewers claimed me off waivers and assigned me to their AAA team in Denver, Colorado. I hoped this change of scenery would be the change I so desperately needed to flip the script. I would be pitching for the Denver Zephyrs in Mile High stadium, home of the Denver Broncos football team.

After two months of turning my pitching around, I was promoted back to the big leagues. Now I was playing as a Brewer alongside some of the game's greats like Paul Molitor, Robin

Yount, Gary Sheffield, and one of my childhood idols, Dave Parker in Milwaukee.

Despite making advances on the field, I was still regressing within. Whether I had a good or bad game, I always seemed to end the night with some sort of cocktail. The pattern of having some type of beer or liquor didn't strike me as a problem. To me, post-game drinks had become a customary part of the big-league package as I hung out with other guys on the team who enjoyed an after-game drink or two.

By the end of the season, my on-field performances dropped off again. The place which was once a safe haven for me was no more. I thought a return home after the season would help restore me.

Sadly, the effects of poor performances and tragedies pushed me deeper into solitude and more sporadic days of drinking. I highlight "sporadic" because when I was home around my wife Brenda, I did not have the same habits or inclination for alcohol. Cunningly, pride, Satan, nor I wanted her to see that vulnerable side of me. Satan wants to keep us weak and silent. So, he will use our own conceit to keep us trapped alone, while he continues to pillage our lives.

Although Brenda knew of my recent family losses, she couldn't discern my emotional state. Brenda continued her daily routine of praying, Bible studies, and going to church on the weekend. She would often invite me to church. Sometimes I went but most of the time I declined.

When I did go, Brenda's mega-church was nothing like the sixty-five-member congregation I occasionally attended while growing up. Her church ministered to about five thousand members on the weekend. From the parking lot to the sanctuary, it felt like a fashion show. I knew little about church protocol, but I felt the church service was too short. For reasons unknown to me at the time, I did not connect when I attended. Since my mind held onto the residue of death and sin, the pastor's messages just didn't produce a righteous conviction. A heart in the wrong place will always pick up the wrong message. I paid more attention to the people than I did to God. As a result, I left church the way I came; lost and confused.

By the same token, my Bible reading came with a pretentious element not being mixed with faith. Reading scriptures misled me into thinking that I was thriving even while I was failing. Since I had difficulty grasping spiritual truths, I sank deeper under the belief that my hypocritical lifestyle factored into the death of my brothers and my poor performances. The manner in which I handled God's word brought no satisfaction. Once I read the scriptures, I did not receive or apply what I read with faith. Therefore, the words on the page served little purpose and the results were the same as if I had never read them in the first place. This approach is like a hungry man chewing a hamburger and then spitting it out without swallowing it. Consequently, he stays hungry and unsatisfied because he never ingested the sandwich.

At this point in life, I was spiritually starving. I needed the covering and in-dwelling of the Holy Spirit. The Holy Spirit could introduce me to the power that was concealed in God's word.

Regardless of my repeated snubs, Brenda continued to extend the invitation for me to go to church with her. Then one Sunday, for reasons beyond my understanding, I agreed to go not knowing that things were about to change. At a move of the Holy Spirit and the invitation of a friend, Brenda decided to visit a different church in Pasadena, California, New Life Holiness Church.

As we approached the door, the small church took my thoughts immediately back to Morning Grove Baptist Church where I attended as a child. Upon entering the sanctuary, the song *Bow Down and Worship Him* greeted my ears as the four people in the choir sang. I had heard worship songs before but this one carried an uplifting tone that seemed to touch my soul. The words to the song continued to tug at my spirit as we were ushered to our seats.

At the end of the worship time, the service transitioned into the hands of the pastor. As she spoke about God's word, I felt an unusual presence that caused me to fight back tears. As shame came over me, I felt something that was beyond explanation. The anointing by which she spoke broke through the hardness of my heart and exposed my weak state.

Suddenly, my mind flashed back to the night I fought against the impulsive pulling's of crack cocaine. Other acts of disobedience along the way quickly surfaced in my thoughts as well.

I sensed it was the Holy Spirit notifying me of the omnipotent power and presence of God. As tears formed in my eyes, I experienced the urge to stand up but pride and embarrassment stifled what the Spirit wanted to do for me. Therefore, I wiped my eyes, stayed seated, and missed the move of God.

Along the way to adulthood, I had built many surface relationships with men who could have been much more advantageous and meaningful in my life if I had allowed them to be. During this church service, I was on the verge of doing the same thing with God—let Him come in, but only at arm's distance. Although I had come a long way, I continued to wrestle with spiritual maturity, content to stay on an elemental level of faith.

Still, each time we returned to New Life Holiness Church, I felt my inner spirit being strengthened and encouraged. Despite my stubbornness, God was using this church as the place for me to discover more of His truths.

About the fifth or sixth time we attended, the pastor descended from the pulpit and started preaching amongst the congregation. As she walked the aisle, I tried not to make eye-contact with her. Yet Pastor Medlock came closer and closer to where Brenda and I were seated. Suddenly, she stopped and leaned over close to my ear and softly uttered the word, "Humility." That one word was the Spirit of God admonishing me to humble myself. Then, she placed her hand on my shoulder and said, "Kneel." Kneeling is a sign of respect and humility. The power that flowed through Pastor Medlock's fingertips was electric. Her touch caused the hairs on my neck to stand while goosebumps surfaced on my arms. God wanted me to know, He knew of my whereabouts and my problem with pride. God knows us better than we know ourselves. As the pastor walked away and went back to preaching, I obeyed and went down between the pews to my knees in prayerful repentance.

At the end of service, I walked down the aisle during alter call just as I did back at Morning Grove as a child. I cannot tell you how many different church aisles I had walked trying to "get right." However, I can tell you it wasn't God's fault that I kept returning to the comfort of my sin. Lack of knowledge had kept me searching all those years. But this time—this aisle walk—was different. Instead of me trying to reach up to God, God actually reached down to me, and I accepted Jesus Christ as Lord and Savior.

The only way I was going to live out a righteous life before God was with the help of the Holy Spirit. I needed the power and infilling of God's Holy Spirit and so do you. The Holy Spirit is a friend who comes along side, moves in, and never leaves. Men, the Holy Spirit is the power we need to admit wrong and ask for or accept forgiveness. If we listen to Him, He will be there to guide, comfort, encourage, and empower us every step of the way. The Spirit is the reason we will be able to stand and take back relationships and the peace the devil has severed or stolen from us.

As the months passed, our lives moved on and I slipped back into my habit of not going to church regularly. September 1991 was a special off season for us because Brenda was in the final stages of pregnancy with our first child. Despite the change in her body, Brenda did not slow in her pursuit and dedication to the body of Christ.

As we lay in bed, Brenda suddenly felt hard contractions. She cupped her stomach and said, "Time these contractions."

After timing the spasms, she said, "It's time."

"What do you want me to do," I answered?

"Call Mom and my sisters. Tell them to meet us at the hospital."

Next, I grabbed the pre-packed bag and we headed out the door. It took us fifteen to twenty minutes to get to the hospital, which proved to be the easiest part of the trip. Hours went by as the labor stages intensified. Although Brenda should have been the star of the show, immaturity and a disagreement over food between one of my sisters-in-law somehow stole that moment. Consequently, Brenda irritably kicked both of us out of the room. That lapse and letdown in judgement cost me the most prominent position I could've taken, standing beside my wife. Instead of my soothing presence during this difficult time, it was her mother and my other sister-in-law Barbara who stood in during one of the hardest undertakings a woman will ever have to go through, childbirth.

Eventually, I received news in the hallway that our baby girl had finally arrived. She weighed seven pounds, eight ounces. We already had a name waiting for her, Bree Nicole. In the months that followed, I could not believe the joy she brought to our lives. It was more apparent for my wife Brenda. She looked like a little girl playing with her new doll. Brenda was constantly changing her little outfits, taking pictures, and conversing as if Bree was going to speak back to her. Within the excitement of our baby's new life, anxieties over the loss of my brothers started to gradually take a back seat.

Once again, Brenda asked me to come to church; once more, I disappointed her by just shaking my head from side-to-side gesturing no. Unphased by my response, she kept pushing Bree out the front door in her stroller. Inexplicably, I sorrowfully sprang to my feet and with sincerity, I hurried to the door, "Sweetie, this is the last time I'll let you go to church alone." Without turning around, Brenda just waved her hand and kept pushing around the corner.

After that, I kept my promise and started going to church with her every week. However, I was going for the wrong reasons. I did it for Brenda and not because I was looking to build a relationship with God.

Up to this point, I couldn't make a distinction between being religious, following religion, and truly surrendering to Christ. My mentality towards church hindered me from fully connecting with God. Salvation was right in front of me, but I just didn't understand it.

Although breakthroughs had happened—having the new baby, doing better on the mound, and accepting Christ as Savior—everything still wasn't perfectly in sync. Sanctification takes time to mortify the deeds of the flesh, and we will actually fight with that the rest of our lives.

Men, realize that progress is part of the sanctification journey. As one pastor has said, "If you were drinking a gallon last year, you should at least be down to a pint this year." In other words, be about the business of progression. Pay attention to the gradual breakthroughs God allows in your life and don't take them for granted. Be determined to continue to move forward, even if you're moving slowly. Soon, you'll begin to listen more and more to the Spirit of God and you'll start getting tired of regressing. You will start to speak to the devil yourself instead of letting him speak temptation to you. You will start to hear yourself say, "No, devil, not this time!"

CHAPTER 12

Game Changer

Don't copy the behavior and customs of this world, but let God transform you into a new person by changing the way you think. Then you will learn to know God's will for you...
—Romans 12:2 NLT

The catch phrase game changer was first uttered in newspapers in the 1980s by sportswriters who were recounting a definitive play. A game changer can also arise from an innovative idea, event, or medical breakthrough. For Dodger fans, the decision by manager Tommy Lasorda in game 1 of the 1988 World Series to pinch hit an injured Kirk Gibson against Oakland A's reliever, Dennis Eckersley was a game changer. In the ninth inning with two outs, Gibson limped up to home plate and proceeded to hit a game-winning homerun which set off a sound from fans that shook the city. The Dodgers went on to win the World Series that year.

Bree's birth was a game changer that had shaken my state of mind and given me new life. My attitude towards responsibilities as a provider and protector swung in a more decisive way, as facets of family, faith, and future loomed brighter. Late night crying, taking turns getting up, and having to be concerned when Bree got colic didn't dampen the joy she brought to me. As my view on life developed, I began to understand that the game-of-life is not a game, it too had rules and boundaries which must be followed.

Men, we may experience game changing electrifying emotions with our sons. I learned that a father at home will undergo some of the same sensations as a baseball pitcher on the mound. The mound where I once stood as a pitcher had earned the name *Hill of Thrills* because of all the unforeseen challenges it presented. You fathers can probably identify with me when I say that being the head of a family and realizing the weight of being a role model for our sons and daughters, is indeed a *Hill of Thrills.* Regardless of which role I played—pitcher or parent—the scene could turn from amazing to *what just happened* in a matter of seconds.

Although it was coming up to our first Christmas together as a family, I had to leave for Winter baseball in Caracas, Venezuela. If I was going to stay in the major leagues, I needed to keep playing baseball and gain more experience.

Once I had landed and cleared customs, I was picked up by Julian, the team's interpreter, and taken to the hotel where I would be staying. Immediately upon check-in, I asked for instructions on how to call home so I could let Brenda know I had arrived safely, and to give her the phone number where I could be reached.

I had been in Caracas about a week when the winter ball season began. During about the second game, I was put in the last inning of the game to get the last out. Little did I know that the same series of pitches I was about to throw would be thrown back at me.

I quickly made my presence known by unleashing a fastball that rose high and tight on the batter.

"Ball," yelled the umpire.

Next, I came back with a slow curveball for strike one. Still, without a swing from the batter, I followed up that pitch with a sweeping slider that caught the outside edge of the plate for strike two. Finally, with a few shakes of my head and without any hesitation, I reached down deep inside and released a ninety-two mile per hour fastball that whistled passed the batter and split home plate right down the middle.

"Strike three!" shouted the umpire, "That's the ballgame."

After getting back to the hotel and settling in, the phone startled me as it started to ring. I quickly answered it only to discover my wife was on the other end.

"Hey babe," I uttered.

As soon as Brenda started to anxiously speak, I knew something was wrong. Her voice was somber and I could tell she was shaken.

"I am at the hospital with Bree."

"What happened?"

"I don't know." Her crying was uncontrollable. "When my cousin Trice noticed the bluish complexion on her lips, we immediately rushed her to the family Doctor's office. Once we arrived and got to the window, the physician who laid eyes on Bree came from behind the glass, pulled her from my arms and hurried her back. As we hurried behind her, a nurse stopped us saying we couldn't go any further. After a few minutes, the doctor came out and told us "This facility isn't set up to administer Bree's level of care." Therefore, an ambulance was called to transport her to L. A. General Hospital. I'm waiting here at the hospital for an update. I'll call you back if I get any more information or if anything changes.

Over the next day and a half, I received one brief update while more tests were still being performed. So, I assumed all was progressing well. The initial phone call about Bree had gotten my attention, when life followed up its first delivery with an unexpected curve.

As I casually moved about the room, the phone rang again. It was Brenda.

What's going on babe?

Bree had to be flown to Children's Hospital in Orange County by Medi-vac helicopter. I couldn't ride with her in the helicopter, so Trice and I had to drive all the way to Anaheim. Once we arrived, we were told she is in ICU, but I don't know anything else.

I think you should come home.

Okay babe, I will call the team right away.

Although the piercing news got my attention, it was hearing about the Intensive Care Unit that subsequently ripped down the center of my heart like that overpowering fastball I had thrown earlier.

After talking to Brenda, I scooted onto the edge of the couch and leaned forward with my head in my hand trying to make sense of the moment. Once composed, I picked up the phone and had the hotel operator call the team's interpreter, Julian, to bring him up to speed. Hearing the news of my three-month-old daughter, brought about a momentary silence, then he responded, "I must notify the team owner and manager before making any decisions and flight plans."

Next, I started packing. Unlike the batter I had just struck out mere hours ago was, I wasn't going to stand helplessly by not attempting to swing back.

One, two, and now three hours had passed. My suitcases were packed and sitting by the door. Although I was expecting the phone call, it still shocked me when it finally rang. Julian said, "There are only three flights a day to the States and the last flight has already departed. The earliest you can leave is tomorrow morning. I will call you back shortly with details." Disappointed, I hung up the phone and leaned back on the couch.

That bit of information was all the sad news I could bear at the moment. The tears that I had held back came streaming down my face. The supreme power of God was all around me, but I wasn't being comforted. I had accepted Christ verbally with my mouth while not observing and following with my heart. Therefore, God's omnipotent presence and power simply did not bring the relief I so desperately needed at the time. I had put on the persona of a strong Christian leading up to this point with my confession of salvation but I had yet to win the total submission battle.

Since that encounter at New Life Church involving the Holy Spirit, a change in thinking had taken place, but I physically struggled with consistently denying deeds of the flesh.

This critical piece of news about my daughter uncovered another barren area in my life that I hadn't cultivated or watered. My prayer life was dead. I had voiced prayers, sometimes eloquent and lengthy ones, but they were empty words filled with rash promises to God. Those prayers were filled with lifeless words which had never taken root because the words flowed from a hypocritical heart with no intention of fulfillment, change, or connection.

Nevertheless, that did not stop me from praying and asking God to heal my daughter. And although I was now on my knees, I was still a long way from being at peace with God.

After praying, I made several anxious attempts to get an international phone link to home but the hotel operator could not make a connection. After all, it was the 1980s, and phone calls were not as easy then as they are now when all we have to do is pick up a cellphone and punch in the numbers. I had to call the hotel operator, give her the number, and then she would make attempts to connect. Sometimes it took minutes and sometimes hours trying to get a connection to the States.

As I sat motionless by the phone waiting for any piece of news from Brenda, the silence and helplessness started to consume me. I turned on the television instead of just sitting there and allowing fear to eat away at my sanity. My eyes stared at the screen but I couldn't process the pictures. Thoughts of losing my baby girl rendered the picture on the screen blank.

Once again, the noise from the ringing phone brought me out of my stupor. It was Julian telling me to catch a cab and meet him in front of the airport terminal at 6:00 in the morning for an 8:45 AM departure. Fifteen excruciating hours had passed since the initial call. I was finally on the plane and heading home.

On the flight, I put on my headphones, closed my eyes, and laid my seat back trying to relax. The flight from Venezuela to Miami, Florida, took three hours and fourteen minutes. Then I had to pass through customs before changing planes for another five-and-a-half-hour flight to Los Angeles. On this flight, I instinctively ordered a bottle of Sprite and took two miniature bottles of scotch to help settle my thoughts. It worked like a charm because the next thing I felt was the flight attendant touching my shoulder and telling me to put my seat in the upright position for landing. After officially passing through baggage claim at LAX, I was now sitting in heavy traffic. The last leg of the trip in the limo took about two hours to get to children's hospital in Anaheim.

Upon reaching my destination, I felt like I'd just completed the longest trip of my life.

After finding my way to the reception desk in the lobby and getting directions, I lugged my belongings onto the elevator to the ICU floor. Once the doors opened, I nervously stepped out not knowing what to expect. The closer I got to the waiting room, the faster my heart raced. I stopped just short of the glass door, set my bags down, and collected my thoughts. As I turned the knob and slowly pushed the door open, Brenda raised her head, before standing up and walking into my arms. We momentarily stood there as I squeezed her tightly. When I got the opportunity to gaze into her face, I saw the seriousness of the battle in her eyes. My wife needed my immediate support and strength, yet my thoughts shifted immediately onto Bree's condition.

At this stage of the game, positive energy flowing from me to both Brenda and Bree were vital, but where would I get the strength to lift her faith when mine was uncertain?

The time had come for me to go in and see Bree. Not knowing what to expect, I slowly walked with Brenda close by my side through the double doors of the Intensive Care Unit. The constant beeping of monitors filled the air as we walked to a more serene room in the corner. As I entered and made my way over to the little incubator and looked inside, my knees buckled as the strength I had built up faded away. Just like another blazing fastball whistling past me and hitting the mitt, I did not see this coming. Breathing tubes ran through her tiny nose while her little body lay covered under so many wires. I stood motionless, struggling to understand my feelings and what I was seeing.

Before this episode with my daughter, I had cowered alone in low-lit hotel rooms trying to drink my sorrow away. However, on the heels of seeing my precious daughter being attacked, I knew I had to change my stance once again as a father.

Bree's birth had sparked a change in my thinking, now her attack was pushing me to genuinely pray.

Suddenly, I recalled II Corinthians 12:10, that adjusted my attitude. It says, "For when I am weak; then I am strong" (NLT). Without my even knowing it or consciously asking for it, by having that scripture jump to mind right then, the Holy Spirit was helping me draw on God's strength—the strength I needed for the moment.

Next, I started to recall other scriptures which lay unused but ready in my mind. Before this current situation, I had made years of futile attempts to connect with God through prayer, but I kept missing the mark because I never gave my confession and profession of faith a real chance.

In and out of the game of baseball, I had pitched and weaved my way through many tough situations. I had foolishly made myself believe that I could control, fix, and face any of life's challenges. However, this was no baseball game now; this was real, and I had to stand up to and face it with my family.

Although I had overcome adversity before, looking back now, I've come to the realization that God is the One who had gotten me that far in life and it was not a result of my intelligence, talents, or daily pursuits. Because of God's redeeming quality and grace, I had endured. This revelation coupled with honest, contrite repentance of wrong brought me a sense of immediate comfort.

I believe nothing could have ever prepared me for that moment except maybe having heard how my father might have navigated a similar experience. But as I said earlier in this book, my dad never talked with us boys about life issues. I found out late in life that one of my brothers died from pneumonia as a baby shortly after birth. I might have gained some strength from my dad's experience if he had shared how he overcame facing his baby's death.

Men: do not let the arrows of pride and stubbornness keep you silent, alone, and not leading or communicating with your sons. Stop what you are doing, consider your history, and listen to your heart when the time comes for you to share and speak words of wisdom.

We discovered Bree had a congenital heart disease called Persistent Pulmonary Hypertension of Newborn or PPHN. Arteries around her lungs and heart were underdeveloped. Deception and denial had finally pushed me into an isolated and unprepared hospital corner where I helplessly stood alone watching my three-month-old daughter fighting for her life, and my wife battling in the Spirit for Bree's life. This encounter with my daughter was not yet over. We were in for a long fight. However, this critical moment is what made me stand up and stop running from my past failures. It made me see that I was no longer on an island by myself; my family needed me to step up and lead.

Men, we have a great responsibility to teach, train, and prepare our sons for manhood because God has entrusted them to our care. How can we do that if we are untrained and out of position? I'm still learning it's task we cannot accomplish without God. So, ask Jesus Christ to come into your heart and let the word of God release you from the pains of the past and your present. I promise that kind of full submission and release will be a game changer.

CHAPTER 13

Squeeze Play

We are hard-pressed on every side, yet not crushed;
we are perplexed but not in despair; persecuted, but not forsaken;
struck down, but not destroyed.
—2 Corinthians 4:8-9 NKJ

A squeeze play is usually set in motion when the manager feels a late inning need to add a run to the score. For the play to work successfully, both the runner at third base and the batter must execute their parts on cue. The runner must break towards home plate at the right moment and the batter must bunt the pitched ball on the ground anywhere in fair territory for it to have any chance of being successful. Since timing is crucial, everyone involved in the play must be on the same page.

Brenda and I had to be on the same page if we were going to withstand this latest encounter with Bree. At the same time, I was still dealing with the lingering loss of my brothers. Communicating my feelings to Brenda turned out to be a challenge. In any event, I had nowhere to run as the uncertainty of life squeezed me yet again.

In the meantime, weeks had passed since I received the news back in Caracas, Venezuela. The overnight wait, the flight, and now all the hours in the ICU ward had taken their toll on me. I was mentally and physically exhausted. I wanted to remain at my wife's and baby's side, however, Brenda insisted that I go over to the Ronald McDonald house to get some much-needed rest.

The Ronald McDonald House was just across the street from the hospital. Once a child was admitted to the hospital, availability, residential mileage, priority of medical and social needs had to be considered before the parent could become a resident. The house presented parents with the peace and comfort they needed to stay close to their baby without having the expensive burden of driving back and forth home. We had been approved, so the convenience was available for us.

Brenda and I could come and go to the Ronald McDonald House as we pleased. The up and downstairs interior had all the warmth of a home. Upon leaving our room, we became a part of one big supportive family. Each person there not only prayed for his or her own child but also for the welfare of other families.

As soon as I entered our room, I laid across the bed and drifted right off to sleep. When I awoke, Brenda was lying beside me; she was feeling the pressure as well. Her appetite had all but disappeared since we got the news. We had been there a little over three weeks and I could count how many times I'd seen her eating on one hand. The effects of not eating had left Brenda frail and subdued in spirit but she still held on to belief. To the contrary, I appeared strong outwardly, but inwardly I still struggled with uncertainty. I wavered in my faith, but this fight for Bree's life was one I didn't want to lose.

When we returned to the hospital later that same afternoon, the decorations in the pediatrics' ward had changed from fall leaves to innocent reindeer and chubby snowmen. Brenda and I were in no mood for Christmas heralding. What we needed was a miracle. This was also the day doctors were supposed to meet with us and discuss Bree's progress.

In the meeting, the doctors unflinchingly explained the dangers keeping Bree on a ventilator for a long time. Blood clots could form. The decisions that lay before us were daunting. Do we continue to leave her on the ventilator or take her off life support? Should we put her on the heart/lung transplant list when it was impossible to know if the organs would become available any time soon? The medical staff said the likelihood of her coming out of surgery due to her size, age, and condition was less than five percent. After listening to the doctors' explanation of the chances for her survival and further concerns, we wavered at the thought of having to wait because we were already at a crucial point. After leaving us in the room to discuss the matter at hand, we prayed and went to be with Bree.

Without a doubt, this was the most difficult decision of our lives. The same spirit of helplessness that I experienced with my mother at my brothers' funerals resurfaced. However, this time it was for Brenda. Although I wanted to be strong for her, I knew that I was in no position to fulfil that desire.

In the game of baseball, I could have figured out a way to pitch out of this situation, but this was no game; this was real! The only way out of this tight spot was to trust in and lean on God.

The moment for the final decision arrived and if there was going to be a comeback, the time for action was now. The doctors alerted us to what could possibly happen once the ventilator was weaned away and unplugged. The possibilities were either she would breathe on her own or fade away slowly. Without hesitating, I once again began to earnestly plead and bargain with God for the life of my daughter. Next, I fixed my eyes on Brenda as she leaned over the side of the incubator whispering praises over Bree. The scene before me was one of supernatural strength.

"Will you unplug the ventilator?" Brenda asked the nurse.

"Yes, let me notify the doctor and get another nurse to help me," she answered.

After removing the wires and carefully disconnecting the respirator, the nurse gently placed our daughter into Brenda's arms. The only monitor giving feedback was the one checking her heart rate. I was now standing above my wife watching with anticipation for God to miraculously intervene. Moments later, I realized that God's response for our baby was complete. Our angel's spirit had returned to the bosom of God the Father. Brenda was gently rocking Bree's lifeless body as though she was putting her to sleep for the last time. Next, she kissed her on the forehead. I slowly leaned over and hugged and kissed them both. After a few minutes, I took my daughter from Brenda's arms and handed her back to the nurse; then, we stood there weeping and embracing.

For close to a month, my wife had strolled around the pediatric room and sat in a corner reading her Bible. At one time, Brenda looked as though she was carrying the world on her shoulders. Yet at this point, she appeared unbound. I knew at that moment; God was holding up my wife. As I stood there cuddling my wife and looking at our daughter, I once again started to cry and silently pray.

"Lord, thank you for our baby. Thank you for never leaving us. Thank you for the hands that worked on Bree. Thank you for those who prayed for us. Thank you for keeping us during this storm. And thank you for awakening me to life, in Jesus' name Amen."

In each of the five losses surrounding my brothers, nephew, and now my daughter, I tried to be everyone else's comfort. Truth be told, I didn't have enough peace to sustain myself, much less support someone else. I realized that the strength of the Powell family came only from the all-powerful right hand of God. These deaths did not defeat me even though I was weak and not a super strong believer at the time. God upheld me. Anyone who hears of or knows my story should be convinced of God's mercy when I speak of His goodness. I don't care what you are going through, God can keep you from falling. No matter what comes your way, God's grace is sufficient to keep you afloat, even in death.

At that moment, I was reminded of Jesus' prayer to His Father while on His journey to the cross. He too wanted His suffering to pass. Yet, Jesus finished praying by proclaiming, "Nevertheless not my will but Yours be done" (Luke 22:42). If Jesus in His moment of suffering went to His Father (God) for relief, then where do you think I wanted to go in my time of need? Yes, I wanted to go to my father but that line of support was not yet established.

Fathers, we have to be in a position to hear and help our sons find the relief they need. We do this early with our availability and by communicating life skills with them which will help them cope with day-to-day demands. Mainly, we have to show them how to call on God through His Son Jesus Christ. He is the only source that can remove the burdens and thoughts which arise from traumatic experiences like death, a terminal diagnosis, rape, infidelity, betrayal, or anything else life is apt to throw their way. Despite the pain, I was determined to keep going.

At that point in my life, I had still not learned to connect my feelings and emotions to God. It had been easy for me to speak of faith and God's goodness when things were going well. On the contrary, when challenges arose, I wavered. I did not know how to fully trust God in the hard times, when the answer to my prayer was not what I wanted it to be. When the challenges arose, I was still jumping in with my self-sufficiency and pride. I was Super-Powell-Man, not needing God who, after all, wasn't handling it like I thought He should anyway.

Fathers, we need accountability partners who can point us away from ourselves and back to God when the hard times come—someone we can trust and go to war with when life becomes overwhelming. Perhaps your pastor or another strong, mature man of God could be that friend for you.

And don't forget the importance of having a godly wife. Choose wisely. God said in His word, "It is not good that man should be alone" (Genesis 2:18). He had graced me with a beautiful wife who had supported me with encouragement and strength. At this time, I needed Brenda more than ever and she needed me. If only I could've recognized it then, this was one of the occasions God had sent the comforting and sustaining power of Holy Spirit through the strength of my wife.

That last pitch—the sad death of our sweet Bree—could have easily squeezed me out of the game and into a life of depression. However, God was not done with me yet.

CHAPTER 14

The Relay to Home

The Lord GOD hath given me the tongue of the learned,
that I should know how to speak a word
in season to him who is weary...
—Isaiah 50:4 NKJ

In baseball, a successful relay throw involves proper alignment and the focus of multiple players. The opportunity for this type of play occurs when the batter hits the ball sharply into the outfield or a gap. As the outfielder hustles after the ball, other players hurry and realign themselves to become the necessary cutoffs. When the outfielder reaches and picks up the ball, he then throws it to the awaiting cutoff man. The cutoff man then decides to hold the received ball or relay the ball ahead to the correct base to tag out the runner or to stop him from advancing any further.

Our words are powerful arrows that carry the potential to wound, bruise, or even kill. Yet, if our words are relayed with accuracy and timing, they have the penetrating ability to build one up and spark a comeback.

Men, one of the surest ways our sons will learn about God's power and our plight is that we must pass it down to them through stories and testimony. Tell them about your contrasting experiences before and after God's Holy Spirit showed up to empower you. Psalm 78:1-4 expresses this same idea:

Give ear, O my people, *to* my law;

Incline your ears to the words of my mouth.

I will open my mouth in a parable; I will utter dark sayings of old,

Which we have heard and known,

And our fathers have told us.

We will not hide *them* from their children,

Telling the generation to come the praises of the LORD, And His strength and His wonderful works that He has done. (NKJ)

It had been a little over twenty-four hours since I stood behind my wife as she held our baby for the last time. The time had arrived for me to phone my parents and tell them about Bree's passing. My mother answered the phone and before I broke down again, I quickly said, "Mom, Bree died last night." Mom paused without going into a panic. She sadly expressed sympathy and sorrow that this had happened as we began to talk. Actually, she did most of the talking while I just listened.

I clearly understand why Mom didn't lose total control that day. When you have undergone one traumatic experience after another, so frequently and close together, the hearing of any more shocking news can be somewhat desensitizing. When I hear of a person's loss, I sympathize with them, yet, in the initial stages, my reactions can appear somewhat insensitive. However, that is not the case. Similar to Mom's response, I now calmly listen to others as they share their news before reacting.

First, Mom asked how we were doing and then she went into a mother's mode by telling me, "Everything is going to be alright." She reminded me how God pulled her up from a dark place after my brother shockingly died a few days after birth from pneumonia.

While I sat listening, she unexpectedly shared another testimony she had held on to all these years. Specific details that I called "the relay."

Mom said, "At eighteen, I noticed tiny bumps developing on my feet while visiting Aunt Louise. They looked like chickenpox or measles. Nevertheless, within a few hours those small bumps had spread from the soles of my feet to the crown of my head. As the condition worsened, I was rushed to the hospital where several tests were administered. Afterward, the doctors still couldn't figure out the origin of the outbreak. I remember lying in the hospital bed with a sheet draped over me but not touching my skin because some of the bumps were now little festering sores. At one-point small patches of her hair fell out and there were tiny ulcer-like sores all over my face and body. Later, after days of tests and unsure findings, the bumps began to shrivel, so the doctors released me to the care of Big Momma.

"While lying across the bed at home, Big Momma noticed something new and bizarre now happening with my feet. Dead skin was now peeling off my feet like that of a snake shedding its skin. The Lord had begun the healing process Himself. God knew what was going on in my body just like He did in Bree's. We must continue to trust Him. He is a giver of life and not death."

After listening to my mom's story and going through all I had been through in the past several years, I began to realize the truth of John 10:10 that tells us Satan's mission is to steal, kill, and destroy. Satan had obtained permission from God on several occasions to attack my mother. There were still physical scars that reminded her of the attack. It was difficult for her to leave home because she did not want people to see her with her scars. Mom painted a grim image of a disfigured girl in my mind. However, her boyfriend, my father, was right there beside her. When the time came, it was my dad who encouraged her to go out. Although mom had suffered, she still trusted God. I had never heard my mom speaking in this manner or length. Her words were relayed with focused precision and delivered with the caring power of love.

God had miraculously spared her life on countless occasions. Spiritual forces consistently attacked her health, marriage, children, and now another grandchild. She then said, "Don't let this change you. Keep trusting Him." That part about trusting Him stuck with me the most because I didn't want Bree's death to destroy me. I thanked mom for taking the time to talk to me and share her testimonies.

I saw a journey filled with life's bends and how mom had portrayed a massive oak tree still standing after repeatedly being struck by lightning. The more she shared with me the clearer the moment became. She was exemplifying the resilience my father should have demonstrated to me. Sadly, one of Satan's most common schemes is to wear us down through persistence. He will use any means necessary to steal our peace, kill our hope, and destroy our lives. The Bible says Satan walks around "like a roaring lion seeking whom he can devour" (1 Peter 5:8 NKJ). I was knocked down again, but I wasn't out.

Throughout that conversation, Mom mentioned how Dad had relayed many encouraging words for her to leave the house. He stuck by her through that whole ordeal. After hearing how Mom talked about Dad, I thought about the man I came to know. What had happened to him? Had the persistency of Satan's onslaughts somehow deceived him? His earlier demonstration with mom as his girlfriend was noble. It evoked all the early signs of love and dedication. Yet, over time, Dad's actions slowly changed to disappointment. Had abandonment, the death of a child, alcohol, and life's pressures contributed to the anger, abuse, and apathy he showed us? Throughout all the years, he never shared his experiences with me. His testimony of how he overcame or failed could have provided me with several fatherly dos and don'ts in various circumstances throughout my life.

However, I am inclined to say the main reason for Dad's unwillingness and volatile behavior is a lack of Godly principles and respect. Regardless of whether he knew God or not, a man never has the right to abuse a woman. I had personally seen and heard the insults as a youngster but could do nothing about it. Standing beside someone in a time of difficulty is part of the marital covenant but putting up with unjustifiable abuse is not. Throughout all the drinking, verbal and physical abuse, there were many times when Mom could and should have left Dad. The devotion my mother displayed over the years revealed spousal commitment. Mom chose to hang in there for four reasons: her boys. She was the one for fifty-three years of marriage who fittingly stood over home in unconditional love.

Once again, I found myself in an all-too-familiar position, grieving in the front row at yet another funeral. I can honestly tell you; it never gets any easier. This time was more painful than ever because it was the home-going service of my precious little angel. Brenda and I had lots of support and family who communicated sympathetic words of encouragement at Bree's funeral. Outwardly, I looked fine but inwardly, it pricked down to my spirit and reopened all my fresh wounds that were beginning to heal. I sincerely wanted to honor all that I had vowed to God, but it wasn't easy. God doesn't want us to carry any burdens. God's grace is always available to carry us through troubled times if we just cast all our cares upon Him.

In addition to church and grasping church etiquette, I had picked up the mannerisms of churchgoers along the way. I knew when to say amen, when to raise my hand, and when to stand up to support what was being preached. This is the deceptive lifestyle in which ignorance had kept me ineffectively stuck. My lack of knowledge about my identity in God made it hard for me to stand up and overcome everyday challenges.

For most of life, I had selfishly missed all spiritual relays from God. My visits to churches, attending Bible studies, and hearing sermons on television all fell on deaf ears because I was mentally out of position. I accepted there was a God; however, it was trust in self, combined with selfish pursuits which kept me wandering without strength for years.

Despite my failures, God's grace and mercy successfully brought me through another painful season.

CHAPTER 15

The Taste of Victory

Oh taste and see that the Lord is good!
Blessed is the man who trusts in Him!
—Psalms 34:8 NKJ

I believe one of the greatest sensations in the world is the thrill of victory. There's nothing quite like tasting success. Although I was a starting pitcher, one of the sweetest memories I recall as a player came in the minors when my manager uncharacteristically put me into the game as a reliever. After carefully making some strategic pitches, I finally reached that all-important deciding pitch that would possibly determine the outcome of the game. As cheers from the fans intensified, I stared in at the catcher to get my sign. After a few unsettled shakes of my head, we had our next pitch. Without delay, I mechanically went into motion and threw a cutting fastball that tailed-in on the swinging batter's bat handle yielding a weak flyball to the shortstop for the final out. As my catcher and I ran together to celebrate the moment, our teammates rushed onto the field jumping, high-fiving, and applauding around us. We had just clinched the division title and a spot in the playoffs. Considering everything we had overcome as a team with injuries, losing streaks, and public criticism, this victory was all the more satisfying. Oh what a feeling.

By the same token, Bree's birth momentarily cancelled out much of the bitterness in my spirit due to what life had served. However, the sudden shock of her death ruined that celebration, thus triggering an agonizing cry to God for help. So, God's response was similar to that of a baseball manager. God needed to send in another reliever. After assessing my pain, God knew that Bree's death had forced me into facing the reality that I couldn't fix the fallout from any of the tragedies that had happened in my life. Instead of sending me "in" to pitch my situation to victory, He replaced my weakness with the presence and support of the Holy Spirit.

It was time for me to relinquish my rebelliousness to God's will. For a long time, I had been moving about life without direction. In my search for worldly pleasures, I ignored the voice and will of God. I gave no attention to the warnings that one day, I would have to give an account to God for what I had done in this body as a man, father, and husband. Now, I had finally tapped into the one Source that helped me recognize that winning in life is a mindset and not just an accomplishment.

Dad's Taste of Victory

Following the switch, I witnessed the omnipotent power of God as He restored strength and wholeness to both my immediate and biological family. Since the death of my last two brothers, Dad had accepted Jesus Christ as Lord. That change miraculously turned his life and marriage around. He started going to church and got ordained as a Deacon. Instead of going deeper into a world of darkness, Dad came to the light and finally took his rightful position as leader of the home. I relished and celebrated every victory. There was a sweet rewarding presence from God hovering over our family that I could not deny.

Nevertheless, our physical and spiritual victories did nothing to discourage Satan and his imps. They kept coming.

In fact, that same spiritual connection Dad made with Jesus Christ led him to stop smoking and drinking. Nevertheless, his years of smoking cigarettes took their toll. Dad was diagnosed with lung cancer. We did not know whether he already knew about it or discovered it in its late stage. Either way, the cancer was spreading. Thank God I was in a position to return home during this season of discovery.

Upon entering his hospital room, you would never guess that my father was fighting for his life as he courageously sat up in his bed. Like the next batter up, there was no fear in his face as he stood calmly in the box against one of Satan's top aggressors: cancer. Although Dad was the one facing death, his relationship with the Lord enabled him to inspire his visitors during his first days in the hospital. The power of God also supplied me with the will to pray, read scriptures, and support his personal needs during that period. It is hard to sit by and watch someone you love and cherish go through so many difficult phases of treatment. The scratchy, wheezing sounds that came with the shortness of breath and the constant draining of fluids from his lungs made matters worse.

Nevertheless, the cancer, now at stage four had moved into his lymph nodes. Dad had lost close to ninety pounds. His body was a shell of what it had once been. I could no longer link him with the man I once feared in my youth.

Dad's next trip home from the hospital was under the gloom of hospice. I had the honor of driving him home from the hospital as he leaned back into the rear seat with his head propped on a pillow. Through the rear-view mirror, I watched his eyes unresponsively looking out the window.

At this stage, I could only wonder if he understood what was happening to and around him. There were days at home when I held his hand, read the Bible, told him how proud I was of him and how much he meant to me as a father. Besides the cancer, I believe the worst moment for my dad came when he was too weak to go to the bathroom anymore. It saddened me to see the uncomfortable look on his face when the nurse, Mom, or I had to clean him up or change the soiled padding on the bed. There were days I had to speak to the dignity of Dad's spirit because he was still a man having to be cleaned up by his son.

God's unmerited favor is what kept me going during this time. The awareness of my identity in Christ made me a servant to God and allowed me the opportunity to be a faithful helper to my father's needs. Although Dad did not speak, I still assured him verbally that I had no problem or reservations about caring for his every need.

Throughout the earlier years, the relationship between my father and me was broken. Instead of spending time talking, listening, and learning from him, work and selfish pursuits had taken away time I should have spent with him. At the time, I resented needing to spend time with my dad and I sometimes acted out of rebellion. I allowed unnecessary conflict to come between us because I held on to resentment and bitterness.

I am so thankful to God that I had the opportunity to willfully express my forgiveness and sentiments to dad while he was still very much coherent and alive. You would be amazed at how simple phrases like, "I am sorry, I forgive you, I need you, I messed up, or I love you" can heal or restore a hurting relationship and confuse Satan.

The act of apologizing healed our relationship long before cancer had a chance to permanently ruin it. Things would have been worse for me if I had waited until Dad was in this critical medical state or placed in a casket before trying to make peace. If Satan had managed to keep Dad and me ignorant of the Bible, that snake—the enemy of our souls—could have stolen our peace and souls from the kingdom of God, thus enlarging the population of Hell.

Fathers, regardless of who is at fault in your present relationships, pick up the phone, or car keys right now, and make the first move to seek peace while doable. Sons, stop waiting for your dads; you also have the power to initiate a peace offering just as I did.

In short, true relationship victory can only be achieved if there is forgiveness. Forgiveness doesn't mean we have to hang out or that we even need to speak daily with the other person. It means we choose to let go of the matter between us, so God the Father in heaven can forgive us (Matthew 6:14). Forgiveness releases us from the emotional influences that internally eat at us, so we can keep the line of communication open.

So, be strong enough to ask God for help before it's too late.

When Dad had been home from hospital for about eight days, I walked through his room to check on him. I noticed this lifeless look on Dad's face that sent me into a panic. As I rushed to the phone to dial 911, my heart rate changed causing my eyes to start watering. As soon as I heard the operator's voice, I blurted out, "We need an ambulance, my father seems to be having trouble breathing."

The operator took all my information and said, "The ambulance is on the way."

When the paramedics arrived, steps were taken to record his vitals but no urgency. It wasn't until I asked them to transport him back to the hospital that preparations for transport and the pace picked up. Just before the back doors to the ambulance were closed, one of the emergency medical technicians asked, "If your father's heart stops along the way, should we resuscitate?"

Without hesitation, I answered, "Yes, absolutely."

Next, I rushed back into the house where Mom was gathering her belongings. Then we got into the car and sped off just minutes behind the ambulance.

After arriving at the hospital, we were told to take a seat and wait. When we got a room update about 30 minutes later, we hurried up the elevator only to check in and wait once again for the consent to go inside.

Moments later, Dad's doctor came into the waiting room and called me outside for a private chat. Looking directly at me, he began to fervently remind me of Dad's DNR (do not resuscitate) wishes. The doctor was right because we had asked my father earlier in his hospital stay if his heart stopped, would he want to be resuscitated. Dad's answer was "no." That was his legal consent. Nevertheless, when the EMT asked me that question back at the house, Dad's prior wishes never entered my mind. All that went through my mind was this couldn't be the end of the game for him.

Next the doctor said, "You can go in for a moment while new orders are being submitted to return your father home. You won't be able to stay long because of the other patients in same area separated from your dad only by the curtains."

We adhered to the doctor's instructions, went in to sit with Dad for about thirty minutes, and then we had to return to the waiting area. There we sat for about an hour or so before the doctor came out with a different tone.

"Your father is suddenly starting to fade. If anyone wants to say goodbye, the time has arrived."

At that moment, God gave Mom and me the strength to go back in and sit beside Dad. As the doctor pronounced him dead and turned off the monitors, I reached over and closed his eyes.

On April 24, 2004, Dad died due to the result of a fierce pitch called lung cancer. No matter how difficult this was for us, God did not let Dad finish his game alone. Until it was time for him to be taken out of this game called life, Jesus strengthened Mom to sit by and pray for him day and night.

As you can imagine, on Thursday, April 29, 2004, co-workers, friends, and family filled Morning Grove Baptist Church to capacity. Dad's friends spoke about his change, his dedication to work, and his love for his family. God did not leave us without a witnessing testimony that day. My faith in God also enabled me to stand up and speak words of change at his funeral.

Along his journey, Daddy had made the transition to my father. He exited the field that day having truly tasted victory having accepting Jesus Christ as his Savior.

There is one more thing about my father that made an enormous impression on me. Although his demonstration of love and trust was questionable at times, when Dad died, he made sure

Mom would be taken care of financially in his absence. Dad had left her as a beneficiary on several policies. He did not leave her penniless having to bear the burden of endless bills. Although he was gone, he had lived up to that part of supporting his wife.

Unfortunately, countless men leave this world without taking care of the family they leave behind. In addition to not taking care of their wives, we still have men who are making babies, but failing in their roles of being a father, provider, and protector to their sons. This oversight is what keeps the door open for spiritual wickedness and curses to keep flowing down into the next generation.

In short, God is waiting for us men to stand up at home and break that cycle. All we must do is ask Jesus Christ to come into our life as Savior. Then give Him the broken pieces of our lives so He can make us whole. Once we're complete in Him, He can guide us in how we are to be godly husbands and fathers.

Regardless of the hardships and setbacks we face in life, we are still expected to live and bring glory to God.

Mom's Taste of Victory

After Dad's death, my wife and I tried to persuade my mom to come live with us in California, but she adamantly refused to leave Norman Park, Georgia. She continued to live on her own for close to four years before being diagnosed with a form of dementia called sundown syndrome. The later it got in the evening hours, the more agitated she became. As a result, my cousins started picking up Mom in the afternoon and taking her to their homes to stay overnight. That was a good gesture on their behalf, but this was my mom and if anyone was going to be driven to action, it should have been me. So, Brenda and I agreed I would go back home with every intention of bringing Mom back to live with us in California.

Days leading up to my departure, I shared my date to return home with a client while training his son. He was the first client I had mentioned that a possible schedule change was forthcoming. After hearing my plans of becoming caretaker for my mother, he did something unexpected at the end of the lesson.

He said, "I have millions of extra points and travel miles accumulated from past business trips and vacations. I want to redeem some of those points for two first-class tickets for you to go and bring your mom back to California."

"Thank you, but I can't let you do that."

"I insist." His resolve was unwavering.

My eyes teared up as I hugged and thanked him for his gift. There are days I still call him to thank him for his kindness. I will never forget him.

In a matter of days I was back home in Norman Park with mom. The doctor's latest written diagnosis of her dementia, her poor vision, and her other medical challenges made it easy for me to retain power of attorney.

Over the next three to four days we notarized all medical consents, paid bills, and administered all legal matters concerning me becoming executor of her estate. Finally, I held an estate sale and gave what was left over to relatives. I was both stunned and excited Mom never put up any resistance when it was time to leave Georgia.

Mom had never flown on an airplane, so there was no way I was going to put her on the smaller plane out of Albany to Atlanta. So, I rented a car locally and we drove up to Atlanta for our scheduled departure. The drive combined with preflight airline assistance at the airport presented no snags. To top it off, we had two first class seats just steps away from the bathroom if needed. During the whole flight, Mom did not have one upsetting moment. To this day, that flight has been one of the smoothest plane rides I've ever taken. Thank God.

It was a major adjustment having Mom staying with us, but the kids had a part of their grandmother and Brenda had a piece of her mother-in-law. I said a part of Mom because the dementia had completely altered her personality. Her challenges got more extreme over a couple of years as the hallucinations and over-night anxieties worsened. Mom's hallucinations caused her to think people were trying to get into the room or that water was rising from the floor. There were times in the early AM hours when I needed to go down and get into bed with her because she kept screaming at imaginary people she thought were under the bed. That helped a little. However, it didn't stop her from seeing things. Brenda and I both had good and bad days with Mom. She eventually stopped taking off her clothes and started sleeping with her shoes on while in bed. Over time, I put a baby monitor in her room to hear her movements and activities.

Although Brenda did things graciously, sometimes Mom's aggression placed Brenda at the center of verbal attacks and insults. I thank God for His grace that covered my wife and our marital union during this time.

Without God, the strain of housing an ill or aging parent could have easily destroyed the marriage. This undertaking with Mom was also a victorious demonstration of love for our kids to witness. They were able to see the level of patience and care we showed Mom. Above all, I was able to still care for Mom. God made it possible for us to give her all the care she needed. That fact alone overshadowed any challenge we encountered.

In May of 2012, we had just returned from the wedding of my son Dennis Jr. I took Mom into her room so she could change her dress. Then I went upstairs to change also. Upon my return to Mom's room moments later, I heard some moans. I rushed in to find Mom on the floor next to her bed. She was trying to stand herself up, and it seemed like her fall had been caused by her hand slipping off the dresser. As I picked her back up and laid her onto the bed, she moaned with pain. Not being able to calm her or pinpoint the pain, I called 911. Once at the hospital, we discovered she had fractured her hip.

Over the next five months and without returning home, Mom was transferred to two different hospitals and two rehabilitation facilities. Since she required a higher level of care and was susceptible to falling, I had to painfully place her into a convalescent home.

After looking around and visiting a few homes, we found one about four miles away from our house. Mom was close enough so that I or someone else in the family could stop by every day to visit with her.

On October 14, 2012, Brenda, the kids, and I went to church as accustomed. That day, I accidentally left my phone in the truck. After church ended, Brenda asked to stop by the grocery store on the way home. While she was inside, I impulsively turned on my phone to a wave of missed calls and messages from the nurses at the convalescent home saying Mom had to be transported to hospital.

As I was about to exit the truck to get Brenda, she walked out. I yelled, "Hurry Mom had to be taken to hospital."

We rushed to the emergency room but we were too late. The doctor came and told us attempts were made but Mom died sometime during worship service. Although I was in shock, it deadened me that I didn't get the chance to say goodbye. Graciously, the staff allowed me some time in the little room where efforts had been made to save her. A covered gurney stood amidst several medical devices. Upon pulling the sheet back, there was Mom's lifeless body with parts of a resuscitation tube still attached around her mouth. Although she wasn't truly there, it was my chance to say farewell to the body that housed the spirit of the woman whose heartbeat I had heard from the inside.

Upon leaving the hospital, we instinctively went by the convalescent home which was just across the street to pick up any of Mom's belongings and to say thank you to the staff. While there, a couple of the nurses wanted to speak with us about Mom's last morning.

"Ms. Powell uncharacteristically agreed to come down to the dining room to eat this morning. Once she finished eating, she slumped her head as though she was going back to sleep. So, we went to prepare for the morning medication round. When we returned and got around to Ms. Powell, I gently walked over and touched her shoulder only to get no immediate response. After shaking her a little harder, Ms. Powell faintly looked up and peacefully said, "I got to go now," and slumped her head. That's when we issued a code blue to resuscitate but were unsuccessful in regaining a pulse. Still, ambulance transport rushed her over to emergency at the hospital."

The nurse's recollection gave me some comfort because Mom was able to leave me a message that it was time for her to go.

No matter what we get in this world, it all belongs to the Lord. Our children, parents, or possessions, it all belongs to Him. We love our family members, but we have to remember that we will have to let people go when it's their time. God alone has the final say in any matter.

At Abundant Living Family Church, I had an intimate home-going service in the chapel for Mom. We had friends and church family members there to support us. Yet, just like at all the other funerals, I buried the grief as I found myself sitting in the front church pew of yet another memorial. Nevertheless, this death did not send me spiraling like the others because of my relationship with Christ.

Today, I can think of my mother, father, brothers, nephew, and baby without being thrown into confusion and despair. Thanks to Christ in my life, I realize I don't have to spend my time here on earth being dominated by temptations and life's curves. Even with the tragedies, I can accurately share the Gospel because I have tasted a victory that cannot be taken away. No matter what trials come, my prayer is that I never forget the sweet, wonderful victories God has granted me and my family over the years.

CHAPTER 16

Run It Again

You must warn each other every day,
while it is still "today," so that none of you will be deceived
by sin and hardened against God.
—Hebrews 3:13 NLT

Spring training is the time of season when managers, coaches, and players work hard to get on the same page. During this time, there were days we practiced the same play over and over again until each player executed his part flawlessly. At the end of each attempt, the coach would instinctively yell this familiar phrase that had become a standard cry in the world of sports: "Run it again." Once we heard those words, each player returned to his original position and we re-ran the same play from the beginning. At the end of the day, this approach put our team in a better position for success.

I had successfully reached the professional ranks of baseball, and it had basically taken me this long before the run-it-again method took hold in my life. Growing up, Dad did not train us boys in this manner. My brothers and I had made it the best we knew how. The repetitive voices I followed were those of my own fleshly desires and the tempting influences of Satan—the enemy of my soul. Oh believe me, I ran *those* plays over and over again!

Since Satan's arrival in the Garden of Eden, he has been recycling and spreading the same old tactical lies throughout the earth with much success. Men have been lured out of their homes and into depressing darkness filled with drinking, drug use, womanizing, and anger because the devil had assigned one of his subtle, demonic spirits to their lives. My dad was not exempt.

Unfortunately, when Dad tried to live, lead, and move the family ahead without God's input, he made an already challenging task all the more difficult. Godly leadership that should have been modeled by morality was missing. A lack of familiarity concerning scriptures and the power that comes from a Godly relationship rendered my father incapable of being able to pass to us what we needed. We, and other men in my lineage, were caught in Satan's web of deception—we thought we were being strong men, when in reality, we were weak to what God needed us to do for our families, and especially for our sons. This spiritual absence from our youth made not only the road to adulthood more challenging but created an inability to pass along godly principles to our sons because we didn't know any.

I truly didn't recognize how recklessly I had been living leading up to my coming to know Christ. That realization came years after retirement when a fan asked me to autograph some baseball cards. Once I was done, the man handed me some extra cards to keep for myself. I thanked him and went on my way.

Sometime later, I flipped over one of the cards to the statistical side like I had done countless times before. That's when my eyes inexplicably locked-in on my journey and the years where my earned run average (ERA) reached its highest mark. In baseball terms, a high ERA is a bad thing. That number means I was allowing batters to reach base and score at an above normal pace. Never before had I noticed that my high ERA marks happened in the 1989-91 seasons, the same timeframe in which the incarceration and life-changing losses of my brothers took place. Recalling those core memories helped me detect three of Satan's most subtle snares—debt, death, and dysfunction.

To start, debt can have a traumatic effect on a man's heart if his heart is not guarded primarily because supporting the family is a vital part of the man's DNA. When there is not enough of something in the house, men will sometimes see it as personal failure. Men have taken flight because they were not strong or wise enough to stay with their families to fight through a monetary deficiency. When fleeing, they unknowingly leave the doors and gates of their hearts wide open for spiritual arrows of anger, abuse, infidelity, and depression to move in and down to the next generation. Consequently, the deserted children will sometimes feel abandoned, especially the sons. When men fail to communicate their mental state after a loss, they run the risk of being manipulated and captured by Satan.

My dad struggled with debt, my uncles struggled with debt, heck, it seemed like all the adult men I knew were struggling with debt. I even struggled with the problem of not having enough money while I was in the minors. In turn, men end up working long hours away from home, which means they were away from their wives and children too. The pressure can seem unbearable and then here comes the snakes—Satan and his imps—to cunningly suggest that comfort can be found in a bottle, drugs, or the arms of another woman.

Next, there is another trap that is just as deadly as debt, and that is dysfunction.

Dysfunction is a common theme for sons when dads—their coaches for life—do not take the time to consistently communicate, train, and go over details concerning life and expectations. Sadly, my father didn't have the opportunity to hear the echoing cry of his father saying, "Let's run that again, son." Therefore, deficiency and disconnect followed him into fatherhood. A man will sometimes become emotionally isolated after suffering physical or financial losses because he doesn't confront the root of the issue and is thus plagued by feelings of inadequacy. That's when pride, that stubborn emotion, keeps him bound and cries internally, "Everything is under control, you don't need any help." Had the lack of money, the death of his mother, the loss of a son, and the lack of fatherly interaction become the root of bitterness for my dad? It's almost clear to see what triggered his abusive and neglectful sides? I will never know for sure because Dad didn't share his feelings or show any vulnerability.

I didn't wish for dysfunction to enter my home either, but it did. For example, I never wanted my children to see or hear me arguing with their mother. However, in the earlier stages of our marriage and parenting, that is exactly what happened. Likewise, knowing how desertion felt myself, I never intended to neglect Dennis Jr. Yet, that is exactly what happened. It wasn't until I sincerely re-ran the submission play with Jesus Christ that my wife and I found success through better communication and accountability. Over time, Dennis Jr. and I finally got the opportunity to re-run our father-son connection. This time we made all the right moves and got the relationship correct through truthfulness and forgiveness. Thankfully, I had learned from my mistakes with Dennis Jr. and was able establish that necessary father-son relationship and speak into the lives of our other sons as they came along.

The third pitfall Satan uses to capture a deserted son or father is death.

Although Christ took the sting out of death, the sheer thought or loss of the deceased can have a lingering, cancerous effect on the survivor if the grief isn't confronted. Sadly, Satan will prey on men's unexposed pain and weaknesses causing him to hurt himself or others. Grief becomes the tool Satan uses to further escalate the men's aches as he makes bad choices. Actually, Satan wants men to foolishly blame God for the death when the truth is that God came to give life, not take it. Sure, we may have days of regret and disappointment after a loss. Yet, Jesus' death and resurrection on the cross is more than capable of giving us back joy for pain and beauty for our tears.

For a long time, I had been repeatedly pushed and squeezed into a painful cell of sorrow. I cowered as a captive behind bars of excuses, silence, alcohol, and pride. It was during these isolated experiences hosting death that I learned some valuable lessons.

Lesson One: In God, we are never alone.

First, I was never alone. God was always speaking. Sadly, I was in the wrong position and frame of mind to hear Him. God is speaking right now; can you hear Him? He wants to show you His true purpose for your life. His plan is to prosper you and give you hope. You just need to listen to His Holy Spirit.

God had given me the ability to overcome the early negative comments critics hurled at me when I was young, however, those five significant deaths in less than eight months sent me on quite an emotional trip. At the end of the day, my view from the front pew of each church and funeral that I attended cast this revealing light off the dark walls of my mind: God was with me despite my pain.

Lesson Two: Our actions can hurt others.

I recalled the scene at Calvin and my nephew's funeral that proved to me that our actions do hurt others. Unfortunately, Calvin's last choice—to pass that car on a blind hill—had caused the pain we were all experiencing. If Satan can get men to think only of themselves, he gets them moving toward destruction.

Lesson Three: Time and chance happens to anyone.

Then, at Benny Lee and Jimmy's funeral, I realized that the race is not to the swift nor the battle is for the strong…, but time and chance happens to them all (Ecclesiastes 9:11, NKJ). What happened on the day of their accident wasn't their fault. We can't explain it, but it was simply their time. Our responsibility is to live each moment in God's will so that whenever our time may be, we will be ready and have no regrets.

Lesson Four: Life is short.

Next, it was the view from where I stood watching my daughter fighting for her life in the hospital and then seeing her in that casket which revealed to me the shortness of life. What bad choices or sins had Bree committed? None.

Lesson Five: People can change.

The virtue I received after closing my dad's eyes in victory was that people can change. Although Dad had made many mistakes and sometimes struck out as a father, he finally got it right through submission and by receiving Christ as his Savior. My dad's transformation highlights the fact that our game versus life isn't over until God says it's over. Don't let a few mistakes—or many mistakes—stop you from tasting the victory God has for you.

<u>Lesson Six: Love covers a multitude of sins.</u>

Finally, Mom's passing confirmed the scripture, love covers a multitude of sins. Although my father, brothers, and I were far from perfect, she gave our faults to God and loved us through them all. I know there are a lot of things Mom never revealed about Dad to protect and cover his image. She could have never stood the trials of time without God's unconditional love and grace being present inside her heart and neither can you.

Men, there will be times on this journey when we will have to run it again with our family to repair mistakes that never got addressed the first go-around. Whether you're trying to fix a mistake with your son(s) or mend the relationship with your wife, it's time to stand up and take your rightful place as the head of your home. Apologize—after all, an apology opens the door for communication. Address any abandonment issues with your son by paying him a visit, sending a card, or simply getting on the phone.

In my own state of affairs with my father, I was the one who functioned as the older man by calling him to the table and releasing him from his cell of pain through apology. It doesn't matter who does the initiating, as long as healing and reconciliation can take place.

There may be moments during the exchange when you must admit or hear hurtful truths about yourself. Nevertheless, God's grace is sufficient for whatever you might need. Let's break the generational curses that have ensnared so many of our young men. These curses have left our sons to fend for themselves—curses which have left them incarcerated behind walls of resentment, pain, and un-forgiveness. Dads, we can be reunited with those whom we love, if we would just stand up and let the Holy Spirit take charge of our lives and actions.

For a long time, I had paid no attention to the burning arrows of grief which were aflame in the walls of my heart and mind. I had walked down the middle aisles of churches in search of Jesus on countless occasions. Each time I got it wrong because after I approached Him, I didn't want to surrender my will or life to His will. Consequently, I kept making the same mistakes and then blaming others. Although, the mere acceptance of Christ didn't stop the attacks from coming, the spiritual seeds that were planted by others in prayer kept me anchored in God's love until I made the choice to consistently follow righteousness.

In fact, I have learned how to break my Christian walk down similar to my on-field approach. In baseball, I learned to break a game down to one inning, one batter, and one pitch at a time. Now in life, it is one day, one hour, one minute, and one second at a time. This approach keeps me in the moment as I strive to make my heavenly Father proud.

Regardless of my past failures and triumphs, I must get up every day and run the game of life again. There are so many family members and friends which must be reached with the gospel.

Right before all the unforgettable deaths and the gross darkness which showed up in my life, God had already positioned people in my path who would divinely point me to Him. There is one who really stands out in the form of my wife.

God has and continues to use Brenda, not only as a helpmeet and friend but also as a beacon of encouragement. If I were going to successfully get ready and break the pattern of neglect that had plagued my family for years, my wife and I had to come together as a team in Christ. From day one, she has never stopped praying for me and my reputation.

Years ago, many of our acquaintances were under the impression that we were making a terrible mistake when we got married. Brenda's friends had grouped me with all the other athletes who like to play games with women. I also received many similar comments from my peers but their criticism was based more on the weight of settling down or being sincere to one woman. Their notion was the marriage wouldn't last. At the writing of this book, we have now been married for thirty-four years and counting. Any time Jesus Christ is placed in the middle of two lives holding the marital covenant together, nothing will able to separate the two if the couple allows the Holy Spirit to govern their marriage.

For the record, that same sentiment holds true concerning a man's acceptance and engagement to Christ. Once he accepts Jesus Christ as Lord, Satan and his imps are always standing daily in opposition, telling him it will not last. Don't let any person, hardship, or evil spirit separate you from God's love.

Despite all that I have learned and faced thus far; I would not wish my road of discovery onto anyone. So, for the little boy back in Chapter seven seeking autographs at the Atlanta Brave's stadium, here's some advice. Think again before wishing and wanting to walk in someone else's shoes without knowing first the path he had to take. That little boy's aspirations made me think of the mother in Matthew 20:21-22 who asked Jesus, "In your kingdom, please let my two sons sit in places of honor next to you, one on your right and the other on your left... Jesus replied, 'You don't know what you are asking!'" (NKJ)

After Bree's death, Brenda and I had three more children, so now we have four including Dennis Jr. Dennis Jr. has an excellent job in the pharmaceutical industry. He and his wife have been married for 12 years now and are the proud parents of three beautiful children. Our son Christopher was drafted by the Los Angeles Dodgers three days before he graduated from college. He played as high as Double A before hanging up his glove. From there, he coached kids with the hopes of getting back into professional baseball as a coach. Today, he is a Rookie league pitching coach in the Minnesota Twins organization. Evan, our beautiful daughter, has finished college with her master's degree and is now working as a social worker. Bryce, our youngest son is a senior in college. He also plays baseball. It appears my love for baseball is infectious. All my children know Christ. The generational curse of neglect has been broken in my family and I pray it will remain that way for many generations to come.

I know God is a faithful Father. That's why He often visits us. The places in my life which were once shaped as some of the lowest points were reworked like clay on the potter's wheel to reveal God's authority and care. Who in Norman Park, Georgia, would have ever imagined the troublesome little boy with the stuttering problem would one day grow and play in the Majors? What about the City Hall where I was once transferred from one police car to the other, being the same place where I signed my first professional contract? Who can forget the baseball field just down and across the street from the Juvenile Center where I was incarcerated? In addition, the dirt road in Norman Park that my father, brothers, and I so often traveled to party, gamble, and drink was paved over. God erased my family's humiliation and pain by covering that dirt road and posting a public exhibit whereby we all could be proud. I am humbled, honored, and thankful to the city officials of Norman Park for naming the freshly paved road "Dennis Powell Lane." Hopefully, the young boys who are growing up in the neighborhood will see that sign as an inspiration to do something remarkable with their lives. I learned that life is not about where it starts, it is about the decisions we make along the way that have an influence on where that life ends. God has mercifully reshaped, restored, and redeemed my life from many painful and embarrassing mistakes.

Even in my family's darkest hours, God's light was always shining but my bad choices and ignorance, mixed with life's troubles, blocked out His presence. Although I wasn't ready, I passed through the waters and the fires of life, and they did not destroy me. I learned in Isaiah 43:2 that God was with me. I now know as a man, "greater is He that is in me, than He that is in the world" (I John 4:4, NKJ).

I hope and pray that you will find inspiration through my story, and that the road you travel will be easier than mine. Regardless of what I have done for Christ in my past or today, I still have to get up tomorrow and gracefully run it again. Men, I pray you will do the same as God prepares you to stand over home providing and protecting your son(s) from the many hardships Satan is going to throw at them.